Developing and Implementing a Corporate University

Jeffrey W. Grenzer

HRD Press, Inc.
Amherst, Massachusetts

Copyright © 2006, HRD Press, Inc.

Published by: HRD Press, Inc.
22 Amherst Road
Amherst, Massachusetts 01002
1-800-822-2801 (U.S. and Canada)
1-413-253-3488
1-413-253-3490 (fax)
http://www.hrdpress.com

ISBN: 0-87425-926-6

Production services by Anctil Virtual Office
Cover design by Eileen Klockars
Editorial services by Suzanne Bay and Sally Farnham

Dedication

---

for Christy, who gives her all for me

Contents

Preface xiii

Chapter 1. **What is a "Corporate University"?** 1
    40 Hours of Training 2
    Levels of Corporate Universities 3
    Why have a corporate university? 5
    Basic Differences between Training and
        Using a Corporate University 6
    A Shift toward Corporate Universities 7
    Learning Alliances 8
    Is your organization ready? 9
    Interview Guide 14

Chapter 2. **Making a Business Case for a
Corporate University** 21
    Industry Analysis 22
    User Analysis 22
    Efficiencies.. 22
    Product/Service Analysis 23
    Keys to Using a Corporate University 25
    Financial Analysis 27
    Key Result Areas and Critical Success Factors 31
    Marketing Plan 33

Chapter 3. **Scoping the Project** 37
    Create the Project Charter 39
    Clarify Team Roles and Responsibilities 40
    Outline the Project Plan 41
    Leading a Successful Project 43

Chapter 4. **Conducting Benchmarking and Comparisons** 45
Common Mistakes in Benchmarking 48

Chapter 5. **Preparing a Strategic Plan** 51
Executive Summary 51
Values and Operating Concepts..................... 52
General Products and Services 52
Key Performance Indicators..................... 53
Alignment with the Rest of the Organization..................... 54
Leadership and Management..................... 56
Long-Term Culture Change 59
Job Design 60
Necessary Competencies 60
Financial Analysis 64
Customer Identification 65
Suppliers and Services 66
Requirements for Customer Support..................... 67
Critical Future Requirements 69
Current Requirements for Suppliers 70
Future Products and Services (within 2 years) 71
KPI Breakout 71
Organizational Gaps..................... 75
SWOT Analysis 76
Metrics Dashboards 78

Chapter 6. **Training and Learning Platforms** 85
The Best Training and Learning Platforms 90
Platforms and Learning Needs 91

Chapter 7. **Knowledge Management and the University** 101
Data Collection 103

Chapter 8. **Aligning Training and Development** 107
Employee Skills Inventory 111

Chapter 9. **Staffing the Corporate University** 113
The Controlled University 113
The Partnered University 115
The Outsourced University 117

Chapter 10. The Small Business University **121**

    Education Grants 123

    Consortia 123

    Learning Model 123

Chapter 11. Conclusion **125**

References **137**

About the Author **139**

List of Figures

Figure 1-1:   Average Number of Training Hours 2
Figure 1-2:   Corporate University Learning Continuum 4
Figure 1-3:   Basic Differences—Training vs. Corporate University 6
Figure 1-4:   University Readiness Assessment Tool............................... 10
Figure 1-5:   Questionnaire for Clients 12

Figure 2-1:   Training and Development Target (model)........................... 26
Figure 2-2:   Learning Continuum Model..................................... 26
Figure 2-3:   Simple Cost Analysis 27
Figure 2-4:   Cash Ins and Outs of the University............................ 28
Figure 2-5:   KRA to CSF Relationship...................................... 32
Figure 2-6:   Create the Visual 36

Figure 3-1:   Simple Five-Step Project Outline 38
Figure 3-2:   Mapping Customer Needs to CSF 39
Figure 3-3:   Project Roles and Responsibilities............................. 40
Figure 3-4:   Strategic Leadership Type Indicator 41
Figure 3-5:   Project Plan Outline 42

Figure 4-1:   Program Assessment 47

Figure 5-1:   Alignment with Key Performance Indicators 53
Figure 5-2:   University Alignment 55
Figure 5-3:   Competency to Learning Requirement
              Front-Line Employees
                  (example of necessary competencies) 61
              Manager (example of necessary competencies)............... 62
              Director (example of necessary competencies) 63

Figure 5-4:   High Level Financial Analysis (example) 64
Figure 5-5:   Customer Identification and
               Code Assignments (example) 65
Figure 5-6:   Suppliers and Services (example) 66
Figure 5-7:   Current Customer Support Requirements (example) 67
Figure 5-8:   Future Requirements (example) 69
Figure 5-9:   Supplier Requirements (example) 70
Figure 5-10:   Future Products and Services (example)........................ 71
Figure 5-11:   KPI Alignment (example)...................................... 72
Figure 5-12:   Organization Gaps (example)................................. 75
Figure 5-13:   SWOT Analysis (example) 76
Figure 5-14:   University Revenues................................. 78
Figure 5-15:   Revenue to Specific Course Offering
               (Strategic Management) 79
Figure 5-16:   Course Offerings (by type) 80
Figure 5-17   Revenue or Course Offerings (by type) 80
Figure 5-18:   Total Revenues (compared to OP) 81
Figure 5-19:   Metrics Dashboard for
               Revenue Generation University (example) 82
Figure 5-20:   Metrics to Include on a Dashboard (example) 83

Figure 6-1:   Training and Learning Platforms 86
Figure 6-2:   Learning Models 87
Figure 6-3:   Skill-Driven Technological and
               Non-technological Approaches 88
Figure 6-4:   Attitude-Driven Technological and
               Non-technological Approaches 89
Figure 6-5:   Competency-Driven Technological and
               Non-technological Approaches 90
Figure 6-6:   Client Assessment Form.............................. 93
Figure 6-7:   Training Intervention Planner.............................. 94

Figure 7-1:   A Basic KM Model 102
Figure 7-2:   Data Collection 103
Figure 7-3:   Meaningful Information 104
Figure 7-4:   Know-How and Knowledge 105

Figure 8-1:   A Basic People-Development Model 108

Figure 9-1:   Organizational Structure for a
               Controlled University (example) 114

x

Figure 9-2:   Pros and Cons of a Controlled University.............................. 115
Figure 9-3:   Organizational Structure for a
               Partnered University (example) 116
Figure 9-4:   Pros and Cons of a Partnered University 117
Figure 9-5:   Organizational Structure for an
               Outsourced University (example) 118
Figure 9-6:   Pros and Cons of an Outsourced University.......................... 119
Figure 10-1:   Pros and Cons of Small Business University 121

Preface

This book is something I've thought about for years. It encompasses years of research, benchmarking, comparisons, and the implementation and execution of corporate universities. Throughout all these years of endless reading and understanding, I've found all universities have one thing in common: they supply information. The way this information is structured and how it aligns with the short-term goals and long-term growth strategy of a corporation is as important as what you place in your university. There is a great need for a book that shows how to design and implement a corporate university that enables execution of programs and learning for corporate employees, which is why this book comes to you.

Today's books on universities focus specifically on building world-class workforces and growing a successful university, but do not address how to design one based on a corporation's culture, needs, and short-term and long-term strategies. Organizational development, human resource, and training professionals will benefit from the strategic and tactical insights in this book. More and more companies are seeing the value and competitive strengths a corporate university brings to the mix, which to me is very exciting. On the other hand, some are creating corporate universities that unfortunately consist of nothing more than a few HR programs and a lot of hope. Many corporate universities provide a great deal of information, but few people use it. Why? Because they can't find and don't know how to use it, but often it's simply because the university is not aligned with any business unit or corporate strategies concerning people development. Why should we expect people to use it if there's nothing in it for them and it doesn't help them reach personal or business goals?

It's vital that the corporate university be an execution arm of a corporation's short-term and long-term strategies. If it is to be successful, it must fit and be accepted into the organizational culture, and be seen as something easy to use that can directly affect bottom-line results for senior leaders and managers of business units. Unfortunately, in many organizations the university is seen only as a cost function; in fact, it should be viewed as a vital partnership with business units inside the corporation, providing personnel information, knowledge management, training, and development opportunities for continued career and business growth.

I've seen some corporate universities fall prey to the "Not invented here" syndrome: if a specific business group didn't invent it or wasn't even asked for specific input, it will perceive the university as a waste of time and effort. I've also come across organizations that will not accept a corporate university unless it is developed by a vendor/supplier, because they believe that the expertise lies there. I can't argue with that insight, but I will add this: There's not a single outside organization that knows and understands (nor has experienced) the current organizational culture, structure, history, and successes inside a corporation as well as the internal employee who has lived it for years. These people possess a plethora of information and should be a key to identifying what can and should be included in a university. They know the political landmines and how to avoid roadblocks, but they also know the "go to" people in the organization. People inside the corporation must be part of the conception, development, and continued evolvement of a corporate university if it is to succeed.

If you've previously read about corporate universities, you know that some of them reside in HR. Others reside in the organizational development function. Still others are autonomous functions—sometimes revenue generators. At the end of the day, it really doesn't matter where a corporate university fits in, as long as the collaboration between HR, OD, training, and business units in the organization remain intact and the internal politics and silos don't interfere with the overall objective. However, it must be "owned" by the corporation's leaders or functional group and provide skill and development opportunities, as well as the business unit's goals and missions.

Workplace learning and performance leaders must continue to expand the speed, flexibility, and rapid execution of learning assets through deployment of Learning Management Systems, business tools, search engines, and technologies (preferably through a university) in order to be more connected to the business unit workforce. Learning transformations will continue to change the marketplace, and corporate universities will play a significant role at least for the next 20 years. These learning assets must reach the workforce, as well as customers, suppliers, and partners so that we can all remain connected in a knowledge-sharing network. After decades of work experience, I can tell you that there's no single right way to create a corporate university, but some approaches will lead to disfunction, missed opportunities, increased costs, misalignments, and failure. This book can help you conquer those dysfunctional approaches and align the corporate university to goals and business objectives, which will help you win.

Chapter 1

What is a "Corporate University"?

What is a "corporate university"? I define it as *a function strategically aligned toward integrating the development of people* within a specific organization. It must focus on personal development, career paths, training opportunities, learning events, human resource programs, and leadership at all levels of the organization. How is all this done? By effectively linking internal and external suppliers, constantly conducting benchmarking and comparison studies of other universities, and facilitating the delivery of the content inside the university.

When I first started to think about the concept of a corporate university and what it can bring to an organization, I turned to several of the corporate universities lauded by the editors of various training magazines and publications for first-hand information. I found out that most of them were not certified or chartered, and did not operate with a strategic plan (e.g., *"We don't have a written plan. Our 'plan' is a list of courses that our people can choose from to help them in their job."*). That's nothing more than a catalog of courses pushed out to the masses by e-mail, catalog, monthly mail drops, or a link into a Web site or portal into a third party site, I thought to myself. The courses are probably useful if the organization did a thorough needs analysis and is trying to encourage people into performance improvement or is doing succession planning or wants to close a performance gap.

But let's assume that a needs analysis is done. Do the courses increase net costs, or pay for themselves? How do you know? I'm sure everyone in the organization can derive some benefit from a finance course for non-financial professionals or a presentation skills course that videotapes participants and shows them how they can improve, but ask yourself this question: Does being better at presentation skills add to the company's profits? It will have an indirect effect if you're in sales, but what about the employees turning the wrenches, making the deliveries, wiring electrical components, or checking out groceries for a customer?

40 Hours of Training

Many companies think that if they offer the "magical" 40 hours of training per year, they're training effectively. That's absolutely ridiculous. What does the number 40 have to do with anything? How does it align people to business goals and objectives? Why do some companies place such a high value on having their employees sit in a classroom for that amount of time over the course of a year? Let's be honest and look at where those 40 hours really go. (The hours in the chart below are averages, based on responses to questions I asked while visiting, comparing, and benchmarking corporations.)

2

Figure 1-1: Average Number of Training Hours

Category	Hours	Notes
Safety training	10	Normally required for all employees. (Don't get me wrong—this is a good thing. Being safe and following safe practices at work should be a top priority.)
Legal training	4	Basic legal behaviors, such as business transactions, ethics, etc.
HR training programs	12	Harassment and diversity. Again, very good training and I wholeheartedly agree that these topics are important.
Off-site meetings	4	These sessions and general meetings are often counted as "training" because information was imparted, such as a PowerPoint presentation.

Participants might actually learn something, but did the training change a behavior? And was it measured?

If not, 30 of these hours have nothing or very little to do with how participants are going to be more effective on the job, because they aren't learning new skills or behaviors that directly influence day-to-day activities, critical thinking, and new approaches.

If every hour of the training is aligned with a curriculum that puts people in a better position to make money for the company, then great, but too many corporations are content just to get 40 hours in. (I'm not sure who came up with the magic 40-hour requirement, but if it's not aligned with employee needs or a carefully developed curriculum, it's a waste of time and money.)

There is no magic number, anyway. Based on their responsibilities and current knowledge, a well-trained and competent employee might need less than 40 hours of training, whereas an employee recently promoted into a management position or a job with higher skill requirements will likely need more than that in order to be effective.

Another interesting fact I uncovered when I was researching corporate universities is that some seem to exist in name only: The instructors and staff wear nice polo shirts and even smell good, and the people who finish all 40 hours are given nice polo shirts, too. But how does that prepare people to face competition, understand the market changes, know which business models and margins are needed to make a project worth the investment, achieve required competencies, make the business more profitable, explain how the corporation makes money, or prepare people for that next critical assignment? Every corporate university should prepare people to do all these things.

Levels of Corporate Universities

A corporate university can be broken down into three learning levels (Figure 1-2), based on the scope of learning activities:

Level 1: Training
Level 2: Training and Managerial Development
Level 3: Executive Development

3

Figure 1-2: Corporate University Learning Continuum

Let's break down each of these levels. At one end of the continuum, we have *training*. A list of training courses does not make a true corporate university. Training is a lot more than simply sponsoring a list of courses. I'm talking about measurement of training using Kirkpatrick's four levels of evaluation:

Level 1: Reaction. Evaluation at this level means measuring how those who participate in the program react to it. I think of it as a measure of customer satisfaction.

Level 2: Learning. Learning can be defined as the extent to which participants change attitudes, improve knowledge, and/or increase skills as a result of attending the program.

Level 3: Behavior. At this level, we measure the extent to which a change in behavior has occurred because the participant attended the training program.

Level 4: Results. What is evaluated here are the final results that occurred because the participant attended the program. These results could be an increase in production or quality, decreased costs, reduced frequency and/or severity of accidents, increased sales, reduced turnover, or higher profits.[1]

Training and managerial development come in the middle of the continuum. All managers need training (it should be identified via a needs assessment), but learning at this level also concentrates on the specific tasks needed to become an effective manager: HR programs, first-line supervisory programs, mentoring programs, and job rotation are examples of the kind of learning that is measured at this level. Programs should be developed to get managers together to discuss and learn from situations others have faced, and what actions or strategies people have followed to achieve success.

The other end of the continuum focuses on *executive development:* the information and skills needed to become a formal leader in the organization. HR and OD usually take the lead in these programs. Planners need to look at breadth of experiences versus depth in the job functions. Career paths are set and succession planning is done at the highest levels; a corporate university

4

used for executive development must be tied to the various programs a corporation already uses and relies on: executive MBA programs, executive coaching and mentoring, and high-visibility projects that executives spearhead and report out to the CEO, board of directors, and so on.

Why have a corporate university?

Now that the term *corporate university* has been defined, let's look at the advantages to having one. There's only one reason to have a corporate university: to help the *organization create a competitive advantage by execution and achievement of business goals and objectives.* Is it really needed? Many business leaders believe that it's important and perhaps even vital, but say that they cannot or will not spend the money to set one up.

How large should an organization be to have a corporate university? Corporate universities have been successful in companies with fewer than 50 employees, as well as multinational corporations, on-site or off-site. It really doesn't matter where the courses are held, as long as the collaboration between HR, OD, training, and business units in the organization remain intact and internal politics and corporate silos don't interfere with the overall objective. In an ideal situation, it would be run in-house and directed by a company executive.

5

A corporate university can tailor corporate programs to the customer's specific needs. Many off-the-shelf programs don't get the square peg in the round hole; sometimes they are a waste of time and money (two things today's corporate employees don't seem to have enough of). But give serious consideration to using an off-the-shelf program as an introduction in a blended learning approach. Just be sure you first identify what you really want an employee to know and be able to do through such a program—it's normally worth considering and worth the investment.

Basic Differences between Training and Using a Corporate University

Training is not the sole purpose for setting up a corporate university. Many training professionals don't realize that there are significant differences between the training function and a university function. Traditionally, training departments are called upon when a training or business unit becomes aware of a performance gap and leaders believe that training will close that gap. Formal training is a way to improve employee and organizational performance and effectiveness, but it is only one kind of learning intervention.

There are others: performance feedback, work processes/design, motivators, performance expectations, new skills, new knowledge, coaching, and mentoring, to name a few.

An organization can use its corporate university to restructure its approach to learning to where it's proactive, centralized, and targeted to a specific client or customer base, and strategically align it to organization goals and objectives as well as specific business unit goals and objectives.

Figure 1-3 illustrates the key components in a corporate university approach.

6

Figure 1-3: Basic Differences—Training vs. Corporate University

Training		University
Limited access (usually a classroom environment) and time-specific	**Access**	Can be accessed anywhere and anytime
Limited to specific clients	**Audience**	Flexible to all clients
Upgrade technical or business skills	**Content**	Upgrade competencies with wide range of available online learning
Mostly instructor-led (synchronous) to include testing	**Delivery**	Can deliver synchronous and asynchronous learning and testing
Open enrollment, manual process not related to any training curriculum or requirement	**Enrollment**	Enrollment based on curriculum needs and online via LMS tied into curriculum and requirements
Typically reactive	**Focus**	Mostly proactive
One-time learning events at scheduled times	**Frequency**	Continuous learning events at any time

(continued)

Figure 1-3: Basic Differences—Training vs. Corporate University
(concluded)

Training		University
Normally associated as a staff function/overhead	**Operation**	Operates as a separate business unit, with greater ability to generate revenues
To improve or develop skills	**Outcomes**	Increase overall performance
Little chance of revenue generation due to limited audiences	**Revenues**	Greater change of revenue generation due to online availability
Tactical	**Scope**	Strategic alignment to business units

A Shift toward Corporate Universities

An increasing number of organizations are establishing a corporate university because they have to. Corporations tend to view workers as a necessary evil—they need them, but hate to pay them. Training and development is also an identified need. Corporations, however, hate spending money on training because they can't see any immediate return—after all, it isn't cheap, and it affects short-term productivity because people are taken off the job to attend training programs. In the eyes of senior leadership, a corporation needs its short-term dollars to pay down debt and reinvest in other areas. How can they do this effectively if the worker isn't there?

Now let's flip the coin over to see the other side. If we don't train workers, how will they perform better, gain additional skills, get promoted, be recognized, and create a competitive advantage for the corporation? This is the dilemma that currently exists in the corporate world. The corporate university can effectively balance the two competing objectives. The university approach allows the worker to remain at work, while the corporation spends fewer dollars on training, travel, hotel, entertainment, food, etc. There might still be a loss in productivity, but not to the extent that an employee has to be gone a full 8-hour day for an extended period to attend training.

Another reason why more corporate universities are being established is that there seems to be a fundamental disconnect between our public and private higher institutions of learning and the actual wants or needs of a corporation. As corporations get leaner, leaders begin to realize that they need people who possess different kinds of skills, rather than sets of specific skills. For example, in the past, corporations thought they would have a competitive advantage if they hired highly skilled Ph.D. engineers right out of college. It worked for a time, but five years down the line, corporations decided to identify and move some engineers into management positions. One day the engineer is an individual contributor, and the next day he or she is a manager with five or six direct reports! To make matters worse, they had to supervise their own colleagues.

A corporate university should provide that managerial training and development while the engineer remains on the job. This allows them to immediately practice what they've learned and get instantaneous feedback from online coaching, as well as mentoring from the person they report to. One can argue that if you want an engineer with managerial experience, just go out and hire them. From the corporate standpoint, however, the organization would have to pay them more, which it won't want to do. Let's take this one step further: How do our higher institutions teach people today? About 90 percent is through classroom lecture, and the other 10 percent is through student reading and maybe a skill practice thrown in from time to time. Yet behavioral research suggests that the average retention for lectures and reading totals only about 15 percent. Again, this points to a disconnect with our educational system. Once a person gets into a corporation, there are no lectures and no assigned reading, but there is an expectation of results—results by *doing* and a higher expectation of *performing*. We are setting our graduates up for failure.

Learning Alliances

Learning alliances are good ways to outsource certain functions. Organizations can jointly enter into institutional agreements, whereby courses and learning events can be put toward degrees or certifications. More and more corporations with reputations for excellence will be offering their own accredited degree programs in the coming years, and eventually they will be considered more valuable than a degree from a higher institution. Why? Because it's in the corporation's best interest to do so if they want to attract the best people and provide them with the skills and performance levels the corporation will need to maintain a competitive edge over those corporations that don't yet understand how such learning programs generate revenue.

Imagine spending a great deal of money to recruit an individual and not being sure you'll be able to attract him or her to come work for your organization.

But let's assume you do hire this person. It's going to take two or three years for this person to firmly plant his or her feet on the ground and take off running. If the company has a four-year accredited degree program and if the student stays with the corporation for at least five years after graduation, here is what having your own corporate university has done for you:

- It has significantly decreased and possibly cut recruiting costs to zero.
- It has cut relocation costs to zero (provided student works and lives where he or she attended the degree program).
- It has provided an education to a known entity.
- The company can release the student anytime during the degree program if he or she is not performing to expectations.
- The student knows the culture and the people and has already taken on projects as part of his or her education (hitting the ground running).
- Employee "students" can be mentored by the best people, managers, and leaders the corporation has to offer.
- The student knows and understands the core competencies of the business, what the company is good at, how others view the company, how he or she fits into the business, and how the company makes money.
- The corporate university is one step in professional development and succession planning.
- The strengths and weaknesses of employee participants are identified early on, so you can arrange for performance development planning and monitoring.

The list could go on, but you get the point. If you are considering establishment of such a program, do your homework and develop a strong business case for senior management. Corporations and institutions of higher learning are likely to be teaming up in the coming years to establish more corporate universities.

Is your organization ready?

Before you get ahead of yourself, it's a good idea to look at what needs to be put in place before financial resources are allocated. Figure 1-4 can be used to help you identify structures and processes that will be required. The items are in no particular order, but the list itself can be used as a checklist throughout the process once you assess your readiness and the organization committing itself to developing a concrete plan.

Figure 1-4: University Readiness Assessment Tool

Readiness Self-Assessment

Is your organization ready to establish a corporate university? This self-assessment will help you determine that.

Rate each of the following statements with a 1, 2, 3, or 4. When completed with the assessment, add up the letter ratings.

1	2	3	4
Not a true statement	Seldom true	Mostly true	Always true

_____ The HR, OD, and Training departments have a positive working relationship.

_____ The CEO and staff openly support and encourage training and development.

_____ Senior managers are able to distinguish between HR, OD, and Training responsibilities and explain how they are carried out.

_____ Employees are able to distinguish between HR, OD, and Training responsibilities and explain how they are carried out.

_____ There is a single point of contact for business units to get information on training/development.

_____ There are clear internal processes in place for training and development.

_____ The organization has a solid information technology or information systems department to support training/development initiatives.

_____ The organization partners with or uses only a few third-party suppliers for training/development.

_____ The need for a corporate university has been documented (i.e., assessments).

_____ The organization has an intranet/Internet site available for employees.

_____ A training function is not embedded in the hierarchy of separate business units.

_____ Training and development initiatives are linked to key performance indicators (metrics).

_____ The organization uses a documented feedback process to obtain information from employees.

_____ The organization uses or has developed a learning management system.

_____ The corporation runs or sponsors mandatory job-related training courses.

(continued)

Figure 1-4: University Readiness Assessment Tool *(concluded)*

Self-Assessment Readiness Card

Date: _____

Add up the number of "1" responses	_____
Add up the number of "2" responses	_____
Add up the number of "3" responses	_____
Add up the number of "4" responses	_____

If you have more "1" ratings than anything else, you have a lot ahead of you. Look at each statement you placed a "1" next to. Why did you rank it that way? What can you do to begin to change it? Who must you partner with or involve to change this? If you try to design and develop a corporate university without trusting and collaborative relationships, you'll regret it.

If you have more "2" ratings than anything else, you probably have a few major problems to resolve. Identify the weaknesses and begin or strengthen the collaborative relationships to address those concerns. The good news is you'll drum up support for the university concept if you allow the others to get in the game instead of standing on the sidelines. Give them a piece of the pie.

If you have more "3" ratings than anything else, you're on your way. It will require very little push from others, but you should remain vigilant and listen. You will still need to establish more collaborative relationships, but the foundation of trust already exists, for the most part.

If you have more "4" ratings than anything else, then you're ready to begin. The buy-in is there from mid-level management even if you're the one who is leading the effort!

The next step in the process after completing the self-assessment is to gather data from clients (Figure 1-5). This will help you determine the validity of your own assessment, and you will understand what the clients already know that you don't. A 4-point scale is best; a 5-point scale normally provides averages ranging from 2.8 to 3.2, which doesn't tell you much (other than that most people are neutral). The 4-point scale gives you information from both sides of the fence. Part I asks questions about how the client currently obtains training and development and how well the training department is meeting needs. Part II consists of questions about what clients want to see in a corporate university; try to develop more questions here, if you can. Part III questions are based on responses in Part II.

Figure 1-5: Questionnaire for Clients

Part I. Rate each of the following statements with a 1, 2, 3, or 4.

1	2	3	4
Not a true statement	Seldom true	Mostly true	Always true

_____ We have a positive working relationship with the organization's Training, OD, and HR departments.

_____ Our senior managers can explain importance of the Training department.

_____ We use the training functional group/department as a single point of contact to obtain information on training and development.

_____ There are clear processes and products in place that show clients how to obtain training and development.

_____ There is a single place to go to obtain information about training and development opportunities.

_____ We currently use third-party suppliers for training and development.

_____ We use intranet/Internet sites for internal employee training and development.

_____ We have a separate functional group for training embedded in our organization.

_____ We use training and development initiatives/programs and link them to key performance indicators.

_____ We use a documented feedback process to obtain information from employees about training and development opportunities.

_____ We use a learning management system (purchased or internally developed) to track and provide training/development opportunities.

(continued)

Figure 1-5: Questionnaire for Clients *(concluded)*

Part II. Place a ✔ next to each item you would like to see included in a corporate university. Use the additional space at the bottom of the form for your own suggestions.

☐ Access to online training modules (e-Learning)

☐ Information about instructor-led courses

☐ Information about performance management programs

☐ Information about HR programs (diversity and harassment)

☐ Access first-line supervisory training modules

☐ Information about career ladders

☐ Competency information

☐ Training curriculums

☐ Six Sigma and workout programs

☐ Coaching tools

☐ Financial training modules

☐ Corporate metrics

☐ Newsletters

☐ Best Practices information

☐ Skill assessments

☐ Articles about leadership and development

☐ Technical training modules and assessments

☐ 360°-Feedback programs

☐ Problem solvers (names and numbers)

Suggestions: _____

_____

Part III. Rate each of the following statements with a 1, 2, 3, or 4.

1	2	3	4
Not a true statement	**Seldom true**	**Mostly true**	**Always true**

_____ I would use a corporate university if the items I selected in Part II were included in it.

_____ I would use a corporate university if it is user friendly and easy to get to.

_____ I would make time to use a corporate university if the items I selected in Part II were included in it.

_____ I would use the training and development opportunities provided by a corporate university for development planning if the items I selected in Part II were included in it.

Interview Guide

Another approach to collecting information is interview clients (customers). Introduce yourself and explain why you want to talk to them. Ask the individual a few questions about themselves, and then get into what you want to discover. The short guide below should help you gather information. You are trying to learn about the customer's concerns and then determine how a corporate university can close the gaps. Note: The term *x-product* refers to training and development—not the corporate university (you don't have one at this time).

Interview Guide	
Questions	**Prompts and Probes for Questions**
Introductions and Background • "Let me introduce myself, I'm _____, and I work in _____. The purpose of this interview is to learn how you see yourself using a corporate university."	• What other careers or businesses have you been directly/indirectly involved in with our project?
• "We'd like to start off by learning more about you. Would you mind telling me about yourself and how your job fits into the organization?"	
• "Tell us a bit more about your work background."	• How long have you been in your current job?

(continued)

14

Interview Guide *(continued)*	
Questions	**Prompts and Probes for Questions**
Customer Story • "What products and or services do you provide? For whom?"	• How well are the products and services being provided to the internal/external customer? • What can you do better? How would you do this? *(Training and development subjects should be talked about.)*
• "What does your organization provide for your customers? How do you go about doing this?"	
• "How do people in your organization learn new work-related information today?"	• What can you do better to help people learn? How would you do this?
• "How is your business changing?"	• Is this based on changing customer product/service requirements? How? • Explain the plan to address business changes and keep people on top of the changes.

15

(continued)

Interview Guide *(continued)*	
Questions	**Prompts and Probes for Questions**
Current Process • "How do you currently learn your work processes?"	• How well does it work? • What problems have you experienced with this? • Describe what you went through the last time you performed this process.
• "What are the pros and cons about the ways you currently learn?"	
• "What should we *not* change about the way we currently learn?"	

16

(continued)

Interview Guide *(continued)*	
Questions	**Prompts and Probes for Questions**
Past Problems • "Tell me about some problems you experienced regarding how people in the organization currently learn."	• What was the most important problem you had to fix? • What solutions did you implement? • What work-arounds did you create? • What was the end result? • What would correct those problems?

17

(continued)

Interview Guide *(continued)*	
Questions	**Prompts and Probes for Questions**
Future Opportunities • "Please explain how you see learning changing in the future."	• Why would a change such as that be important to you in the future?
• "Describe what you see as an ideal way to learn."	• What would that look like, and why would that be important?
• "How can you improve the way employees learn?"	• What would these improvements do for the way people learn in the organization?

18

(continued)

Interview Guide *(concluded)*	
Questions	**Prompts and Probes for Questions**
Learning Priorities • "What are the top five training and development opportunities needed by the organization?"	• Why are these most important? • What would a simple solution (to meeting these needs) look like?
Closing Remarks • "This brings us to the end of the questions. Is there anything you believe is important for us to know?" • "Thank you for your time. May we call you if any other questions come up?"	

19

Once the questionnaire and the interview have been completed, you need to compile the information you have collected for meaningful feedback. This compilation of data should go back to the interviewees for two reasons:

1. To verify that the information is accurate
2. To rank the data you collected in order of importance

Having the interviewees rank the data in order of importance will help you identify areas where the corporate university will be most attractive and useful. This approach also helps you align the university with current desires and/or needs using real data from the people you want to use its programs. Though this may take a bit of time, this approach is the best way to find out what employees want or need in the way of training and development. (Note: This approach is similar to a Design for Six Sigma (DFSS) methodology.)

One final tip: Interviewing employees and asking them to verify and rate information assures interviewees that they are an important part of the process and that you're receptive to their ideas and concerns.

Chapter 2

Making a Business Case for a Corporate University

Much of the information presented in this book has to do with making a business case for a corporate university. This chapter acts as an introduction to the topic. As you continue through the rest of the chapters, you'll begin to make your own determination about what you want or need to present in your business case.

Most corporations have a format for presenting a business case. It starts with a feasibility analysis and management plan. At a minimum, it must include the following:

- An industry analysis (current conditions and industry norms)
- A user analysis
- Efficiencies
- Product/service analyses
- Keys to using the corporate university
- A financial analysis
- Key result areas and critical success factors
- A marketing plan

Industry Analysis

A corporate university is a training and development product that is not normally subject to the competition of external environments such as the life cycle, carrying capacity, competition profiles, bargaining power, and barriers to entry into a market. The industry analysis should focus on current conditions and industry norms. A corporate university is a function strategically aligned toward integrating the development of people. Most include one or more of the following:

- A list of internal/external training opportunities
- A list of internal/external training and development opportunities
- Training and development opportunities attached inside an internal/external learning management system (LMS)
- Training and development opportunities attached inside an LMS, aligned with individual development planning

Standard formats and information contained within corporate universities will differ. The more credible universities that cater to both internal and external customers use competitor information, direct contact, training and development trade magazines, forums, and conferences to help them determine curriculum areas.

22

User Analysis

Since a corporate university caters to internal customers (employees), it must be made available to all business units inside the corporation. If it is Web-based on the company's intranet, demographic profiles, population data, and location availability are not relevant. If your university is to be made available to people outside the corporation, you'll need to complete a marketing study. Some corporate universities (such as Disney University) offer managerial training to other corporations.

Efficiencies

A business case will need to outline the specific efficiencies gained by the user and the organization. This section must clearly spell out what you expect to gain, because some of these efficiencies will most likely be measured and used for performance planning:

- The training courses and program offerings from preferred vendors (suppliers)
- Anticipated cost savings for internal course and program offerings
- Standardization of training and development programs
- Economies of scale of supplier training programs
- Closing training and development gaps
- Potential productivity increase

Product/Service Analysis

In this section of the business case, you define the product. The corporate university is a strategic tool to help workers achieve goals by providing personal development, operational efficiency, performance support, and training tools. In your business case, you might need to say, "It contains a selection of 500 instructor-led and self-study courses, 1,200 terms and definitions, and substantial numbers of job aids and references. It also incorporates a learning management system." (Note: If the training content inside the LMS is designed and developed within the corporation and launched from the LMS itself, you can call it a Learning Content Management System.)

The terms *LMS* and *LCMS* are often used interchangeably, but regardless of whether an LMS or LCMS is used, the university should contain centers of quality that help individuals and teams investigate, discover, and uncover opportunities, and take on challenges. Here are examples of "centers of quality" that can be developed, as well as what they might contain:

- *Personal Development Center.* The personal development center houses links to vendor or internal sites and products. It should contain information about:
  - 360° feedbacks
  - Personality type indicators (Myers-Briggs or DiSC)
  - Input-output processing models (I-OPT)
  - Emotional Intelligence (EQ)
  - Links to leadership-development partners and/or internal programs

23

- *Career Guidance Center.* The career guidance center houses career path information and self-awareness assessment programs that were either developed internally or developed by a vendor. It should include information about:

  — The company's career development steps/pathing

  — Career assessment and next steps

  — Career options

  — Career opportunities within the organization

  — HR help

  — How to create a career timeline

- *Training Center.* The training center focuses on training opportunities in the learning management system. It should include information about:

  — Learning management systems, with a direct link to access the LMS/LCMS

  — Performance support materials (not training)

  — Approved vendor courses and links to sites

  — Company/business unit orientation packages

  — Performance management processes

  — Curriculum requirements (by position)

- *Human Resource Center.* The human resources center houses information about HR programs, such as:

  — Links to policy letters

  — Succession planning templates for managers

  — Mentoring programs

  — Company benefits (link)

  — Competency explanations/definitions

- *Process Information Center.* This center should outline and provide specific examples of all business unit processes. You can break out and link the different business units within this center. It should incorporate things such as the business unit function, how it makes money, key contacts, completed projects, ongoing projects, strategic partners, etc.

- *Idea Center.* This should be a link that opens to a document that asks the user for ideas on making the corporate university more effective, as well as ideas about training, development, processes, and anything else pertinent to the continuous development of people in the organization. It can also include:

  — New ideas
  — Current product add-ons
  — What the customer wants and needs
  — Market research opportunities and functions

Keys to Using a Corporate University

This section should explain how the university is to be used. It's vital that you tie in the statements in this section to organizational goals and program objectives. If you do not establish a clear link, you might not get the project funded.

1. Training and development activities outside of an approved curriculum should be pre-approved by a manager and directly tied to a Personal Development Plan.

2. Not all training and development activities can be provided through the university. Sometimes job rotations, Six-Sigma participation, team interactions, and stretch assignments are developmental *situations* for learning.

3. Areas identified for training and development-related activities are applicable to current or potential development and work assignments, using a training and development model shown in Figure 2-1 and the learning continuum model shown in Figure 2-2.

25

Figure 2-1: Training and Development Target (model)

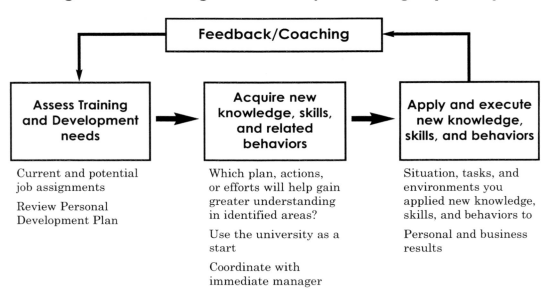

Current and potential job assignments

Review Personal Development Plan

Which plan, actions, or efforts will help gain greater understanding in identified areas?

Use the university as a start

Coordinate with immediate manager

Situation, tasks, and environments you applied new knowledge, skills, and behaviors to

Personal and business results

Figure 2-2: Learning Continuum Model

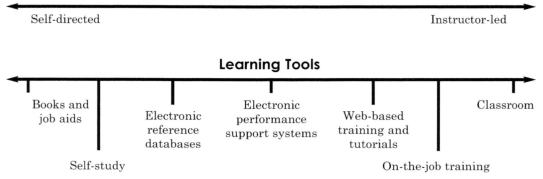

Financial Analysis

Figure 2-3 is a very basic example of the *costs associated* with a corporate university, illustrating capital-project components and non-capital project components, with associated costs in dollars.

Figure 2-3: Simple Cost Analysis

Corporate University Components	Initial Costs	One-Time License Costs	Annual Maintenance Costs	Additional Annual Estimate Costs
Learning Management System				
LMS	$75,000	$8,000	$6,280	
Online LMS			$3,420	
Automatic flow events	$13,000		$3,440	
Testing software	$4,000	$2,400		
On-site support	$2,100			$8,000
Subtotals	**$94,100**	**$10,400**	**$13,140**	**$8,000**
Hardware				
Server (low end)	$8,000			
Subtotals	**$8,000**			
Vendor Programs				
X-Vendor				$32,000
Y-Vendor				$25,000
Subtotals	**$102,100**	**$10,400**	**$13,140**	**$65,000**
Labor				
IT support				$50,000
University labor				$400,000
Other Costs				
Other budget figures (marketing, travel, materials, etc.)				$500,000

27

The Corporate University as a Business

The primary business goal of a corporate university is to make a profit and pay for the resources needed to operate it. The objective of the profit motive is to maximize the profit on the capital invested. To do this, we'll look at several financial considerations if the university is to be used as a source of revenue:

- Cash flow
- Net present value
- Cost of capital
- Internal rate of return
- Return on Investment (ROI)

Cash Flow

Cash flows keep the university lucrative in the short term. A business with a relatively small cash flow has a difficult time meeting short-term cost obligations. The illustration in Figure 2-4 shows the basic "ins" and "outs" of cash flow for a corporate university.

Figure 2-4: Cash Ins and Outs of the University

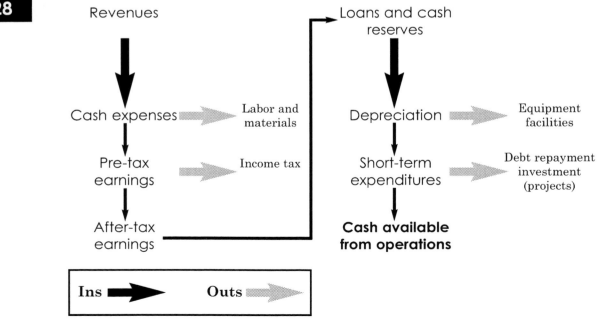

Net Present Value

Discounted cash-flow analysis determines a project's rate of return based on today's dollars. Cash is paid out today to complete a project; in most cases, it won't be returned in revenues until sometime in the future. The longer it takes to generate revenue, the less they will be worth to the business today. To evaluate projects effectively, we need a way to compare how future cash flows begin to be paid out today. A calculation called net present value is used to determine the value of tomorrow's dollars today.

Net present value (NPV) is a way of calculating a project's return on investment by converting future cash inflows and outflows to their present value. The NPV calculation will tell you if the project can return the cost of capital. A required rate of return (also known as a "hurdle rate") is a number set by the organization as a minimum acceptable return (percent of investment). For example, Project A shows the cash flow expectations over 5 years (numbers in the hurdle rate column are discounted cash rates). The organization set the hurdle rate at 15 percent. Using a present value table we get the following:

Year	Cash Flow	Hurdle Rate 15%	Discounted Cash Flow
0	($80,000)	1.000	($80,000)
1	$20,000	0.8696	$17,392
2	$20,000	0.7561	$15,122
3	$40,000	0.6575	$26,300
4	$60,000	0.5718	$34,308
5	$100,000	0.4972	$49,720

Since the discounted cash inflows of $142,842 exceed the cash outflow, the project has a "hurdle rate" of over 15%. The net present value is $142,842 − $80,000 or $62,842.

Cost of Capital

The cost of capital is defined as the cost of an organization's long-term debt and equity—in other words, its worth. An organization should not develop a corporate university that generates less revenue than its cost, if the university is to be used as a source of revenue. The cost of capital is expressed as a percentage and is typically calculated as a weighted average. This can range between 12 and 30 percent for a corporate university, depending on the risk of the project.

To determine the minimum cost of capital for a university project, let's use the example below. Let's say your company's long-term liabilities and shareholder equity on the balance sheet show $300 million and $800 million respectively. The cost of the liabilities is normally the after-tax cost of interest, so for long-term liability, the annual cost is $18 million. The cost for shareholder equity is $75 million annually.

Item	Amount	Rate	Annual Cost
Long-term liabilities	$300,000,000	6%	$18,000,000
Shareholder equity	$800,000,000	9.375%	$75,000,000
	$1,100,000,000		$93,000,000

So $93,000,000 divided by $1,100,000,000 equals 8.45 percent. This is the cost of capital, and is normally set as the minimum acceptance for capital-project returns.

Internal Rate of Return

The internal rate of return (IRR) method determines the project's return rate and compares it to the hurdle rate. Let's go back to our 5-year university project example: We said the initial cash outflow was $80,000 and the 5-year cash flow was $142,842. For simple purposes, we'll divide the total discounted cash flow by 5 years to get an average annual cash flow that equals $28,568. (Normally, the IRRs would be calculated separately). The formula for IRR would be $80,000 divided by $28,568 or 2.80. Consulting the table and using the 5-year line, we look for 2.80 and find the IRR is approximately 24 percent.

Return on Investment

Return on investment (ROI) is a generic term that normally refers to the return an organization gets on project expenses. Let's look at a very basic example (it doesn't include transportation, depreciation/amortization, or maintenance costs). Let's say we'll spend $15 million on our initial university project. We'll spend $4 million on university upgrades over a 5-year period. We'll also spend $8 million in labor costs and expenses over that same time period. The total revenues generated by the university by year 5 are expected at $90 million. The basic ROI would be calculated as:

Category	Dollars
Revenues	$90,000,000
Startup	$15,000,000
Upgrades	$4,000,000
Labor/overhead/expenses	$8,000,000

ROI in dollars is calculated by subtracting costs from revenues:

$90,000,000 − ($15,000,000 + $4,000,000 + $8,000,000) = $63,000,000

To convert the ROI to a percentage, divide ROI dollars by revenues for a 70 percent return on investment.

Key Result Areas and Critical Success Factors

Figure 2-5 helps clarify and identify the key result areas (KRAs) associated with a corporate university and the critical success factors (CSFs). These KRAs should relate directly to the notes from customer interviews we discussed earlier in the book. This is an important section, as it will reappear in the project scope to be discussed later. Key result areas are:

- Use by employees for training and development
- Decreased reliance and dollars spent on vendor training
- Wide range of business unit training offered within the university

31

Figure 2-5: KRA to CSF Relationship

Key Result Areas	Critical Success Factors (Known Customer Needs)
Employee use for training and development	— High availability rates (down time) — High accessibility rates — Use university with Performance Development program — Identify training curriculums for business units — LMS workflow identifies gaps to managers and students — Capture vendor and internal training — Testing online — Compile training reports — Ease of use — Develop feedback mechanisms
Decreased reliance and dollars spent on vendor training	— Get management involved in approval process — Provide a comprehensive list of internal training programs — Obtain information about workers who have attended vendor programs — Identify trainers within the company — Compute cost-avoidance financials — Take advantage of vendor economies of scale — Identify new training courses in the university
Wide range of business unit training offered within the university	— Identify training curriculums for business units — Insist that all business units identify curriculums and input into the LMS — Develop first-time supervisor's course — Identify corporate development programs — Schedule business skills training courses — Schedule technical courses

Marketing Plan

Determining what should go into a corporate university's marketing plan is not as easy as one would think. You will need to answer some basic questions as you begin to develop the plan.

What is our product?

You would think the answer is a university, but it's not. What you're offering as the product is organizational development and training services, encompassing such things as:

- Leadership programs
- Technical skills development
- Cross-functional work processes
    — Six Sigma
    — Lean production
    — Kaizen (workout)
- Succession planning
- Strategic planning
- Performance management
- Supervisory skills

33

What is the product definition?

We said our product is organizational development ·and training services. Organizational development is a long-range implementation of planned change for the purpose of organizational improvement. It's designed to change an organization's culture by using behavioral science technologies, research, and theory.[2]

"Training" is the act, process, or method used to provide the skill, knowledge, and experience a worker needs to correctly and successfully complete a given task or set of tasks.

What is the primary product makeup?

In this section, you need to include the specifics of what the product is made up of:

- Design organizational development (OD) strategies using proven data-driven behavioral and research assessments and/or programs.
- Implement action research via observations, assessments, and surveys to assess and recommend changes in order to attain organizational goals and business objectives.
- Design, develop, and help manage functional and business-unit training strategies.
- Interface with business-unit directors and managers to design, develop, and implement appropriate educational programs to meet business objectives.
- Assess current and future training and educational programs to determine organizational value and return on investment.
- Direct university and associated strategies that support long-term business growth.
- Direct and implement the Learning Management System in support of training requirements.
- Measure training effectiveness data (to include costs, cost avoidance, employee training hours, curriculum management, and training) to Key Performance Indicators (KPI) correlation.
- Provide training material design products and services.
- Conduct sales-training courses.

Who are the customers?

Identify and define all customers. Determine if they are internal, external, or both. Are they grouped into business areas, or do they consist of the whole organization? Do we have an established customer base? Are we going after new customers? What does the current customer base look like? (Managerial or non-managerial? White collar or blue collar? Hourly or salary?) There are many ways to segment customers. No matter how you identify them, be sure you identify them!

What will a corporate university do for the customer?

Begin by addressing known needs, and tell the customer how you'll close the gap for them. Use the statement "We address all of your training and development needs by _____."

- Identify training needs (Needs Assessment).
- Use the Instructional Systems Design (ISD) approach to determine most-effective, least-cost training platforms and/or supporting materials to be designed.
  — Develop training objectives.
  — Design and develop training materials.
  — Measure training effectiveness.
  — Compute returns/cost avoidance on training dollar investments.
- Develop department training strategies in support of business objectives.
- Provide a complete learning management system of online training capabilities, including Web courses, assessments, tests, performance support materials, and training curriculum management via an LMS.
- Facilitate and/or teach sales courses and business skills in a classroom and in an e-learning environment.
- Conduct research to design and apply the OD strategies and employee interventions.
- Determine capabilities of supplier (vendor) training programs in support of objectives.

35

What experience do we bring?

Experience means a great deal. It means even more if you bring it into your marketing plan. Consider phrasing it by using "We bring (list all the experiences your team brings to the table)":

- "Over 100 years of training and development experience."
- "A wide range of business experience in (i.e., human resources; sales; logistics; retailing; procurement; competitive sourcing and privatization; training; and organizational development)."

Create the Visual

You'll find it beneficial to create a visual to help the marketing plan come to life. Figure 2-6 shows how you can help the reader understand what the corporate university will do for training and development.

Figure 2-6: Create the Visual

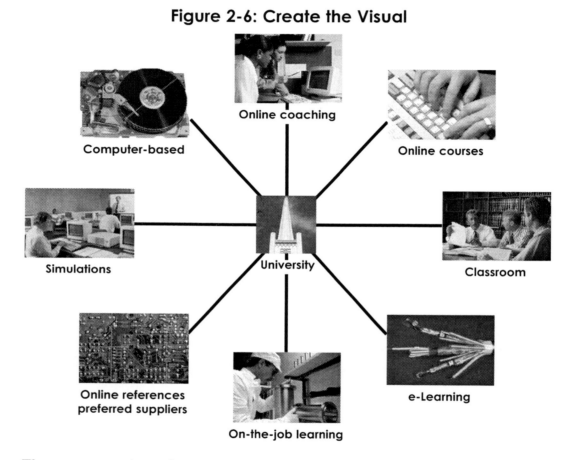

There are a variety of ways to use visuals effectively and a variety of ways to distribute them. Putting something in people's hands is better than sending a link to a site, especially when the corporate university is in its infancy.

Chapter 3

Scoping the Project

The next step is to determine the scope of the project. Several basic principles need to be applied here that will be familiar to you if you have ever done project management. Standard project management does several things:[3]

- It ensures that customer requirements are met.

- It keeps you from reinventing the wheel by standardizing routine project work.

- It reduces the number of tasks that might otherwise be overlooked in the project.

- It prevents duplication of efforts.

- It keeps projects under control.

- It maximizes use of resources.

What if you don't use project management? Teams that do not use a project-management approach experience these results:

- There is duplication of work and effort.
- Team skills are not matched to requirements.
- Cost overruns occur.
- Deadlines are missed.
- Scope of the project changes continuously.
- Team conflicts occur.
- Projects lose funding.
- Resources are pulled from the project.
- Risk of project failure increases.

Avoid some of the pitfalls, and use project management principles to keep the university project on track. Be sure you outline a basic project roadmap using the five steps in Figure 3-1.

Figure 3-1: Simple Five-Step Project Outline

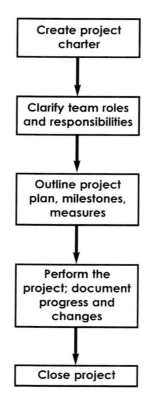

Create the Project Charter

In this step, you must document the purpose of the university. The scope of the project covers objectives, stakeholders, and resources required, as well as what the university is expected to deliver. This last part should reflect what those using its services want, but it's very important that you don't let the "customers" take control or tell you what it should look like. By all means, take notes on their needs, but at this point, you're concern is putting together a charter that will launch the team in the right direction.

For example, let's look at a book on management. What's the most important part of that book? The *information.* We're not concerned about how the information gets into the book, as long as it meets expectations, addresses needs, and is accurate. Determine the critical success factors associated with the customer need, using a format similar to the one on this page. There can be any number of critical success factors for one requirement; insert your specific customer needs and CSFs in Figure 3-2.

Figure 3-2: Mapping Customer Needs to CSF

Customer Need	Critical Success Factors (CSFs)
Access to online training courses	Ability for the client to complete online training courses IT infrastructure concerns, such as bandwidth
Training reports for management	Identify training modules completed
Online registration for instructor-led courses	Register online for courses IT infrastructure concerns, such as bandwidth
Curriculum management	Identify and develop curricula View curricula online
HR program updates	Information on HR programs
Career information and programs	Career paths Self-assessment programs
E-mail reminders about non-completed training requirements	IT infrastructure concerns, such as bandwidth

39

The final element in the charter is the criteria for acceptance, which is simply a summary of your objectives.

Clarify Team Roles and Responsibilities

If you do not clarify team roles and responsibilities at the outset, your project will either fail or not meet its intended objective. Take the time to determine and clarify these important elements, and establish (and use) team meeting ground rules, agendas, and methods for resolving differing opinions, and work out parking lot assignments.

A useful tool for clarifying team roles and responsibilities is shown in Figure 3-3. It will help you identify project functions and assign roles for individuals on the team. If you are the team leader or you are answerable for the university project, you'll want to have the table filled out before your first meeting. (Some roles may change during the initial meeting.) *Answerable* refers to the person who holds the ultimate accountability for the results of the entry in the project function block. This is usually the project manager or project "owner" or stakeholder. *Responsible* means that the individual has the responsibility to make sure the tasks related to the entry in the project function block are completed. *Collaborate* identifies the client/customer resources you are partnering with. In our example on the chart, there are six members on the team: Doris, Ginger, Matthew, Holly, Ed, and Ken. Holly and Matthew are project leaders.

Figure 3-3: Project Roles and Responsibilities

Project Function	Answerable to	Responsible to	Collaborate with
Total project management (Leading entire project)	Project manager: you	• Holly • Matthew	• Team leaders • Team members • Customers • Outside resources • Vendors • Cross-functional business groups
Lead team and collaboration efforts, answerable to project manager	Project leaders: Holly Matthew	• Doris • Ginger • Ed • Ken	• Project manager • Team members • Customers • Outside resources • Vendors • Cross-functional business groups
Lead sub-teams, answerable to project leaders	Leaders of sub-teams: Doris Ginger Ed Ken	• Sub-team members	• Project leaders • Sub-team members • Customers • Clients • Outside resources • Vendors

If you use this model, there are a couple of things you need to be aware of. Your project is not going to succeed unless team leaders all have the desire and the capability to lead the project. They have to understand the scope of the project, team dynamics, and coaching, and they have to be able to manage the project. Figure 3-4 illustrates Alexander Hiam's Strategic Leadership Type Indicator (SLTi) model.[4]

The model illustrates the relationship between focusing on the performance and focusing on the performer. The focus on the performance relates to the difficulty, whereas the focus on performer relates to the amount of interaction between the project leader and the team member. I've just scratched the surface of the model, but I encourage you to learn more about it, especially if you're accountable for the implementation of the university and using teams to execute the strategy.

Figure 3-4: Strategic Leadership Type Indicator

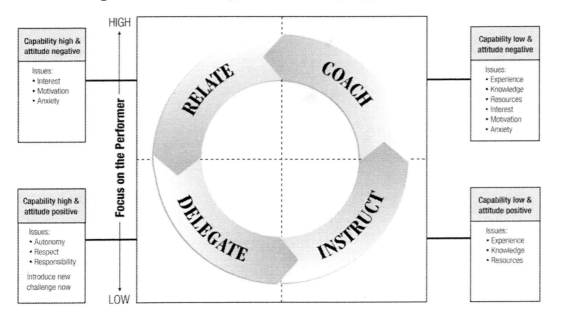

41

Outline the Project Plan

It is time to develop an implementation plan. It should cover activities, deliveries, milestones, and who's involved in the activity. Figure 3-5 presents a basic project outline. (Note: The numbers in the "milestone" column refer to the number of days from the starting date of the project.)

Item #	Activity	Deliverable	Responsibility	Milestone
1	Conduct assessment to determine if a corporate university is needed	Needs analysis (summary)	Project manager	30 days after initial startup of project
2	Assessment of organizational readiness	Readiness analysis	Project manager	Complete within 7 days of completion of item 1
3	Outline project scope and capture ideas and critical success factors related to customer needs	Project charter	Project manager Project leaders	Complete within 30 days of completion of item 2
4	Create basic outline of the project	Project plan (outline)	Project manager Project leaders	Complete within 7 days of completion of item 3
5	Collect information that will be used in making the business case for a corporate university	Business case	Project manager Project leaders	Complete within 30 days of completion of item 4
6	Create the strategies, key result areas, critical success factors, current capabilities, objectives, and goals of the university	Strategic plan	Project manager Project leaders Team members	Complete within 30 days of completion of item 5
7	Identify the tasks required to complete goals and objectives for strategic plan	Gap assignments	Project manager Project leaders Team members	Complete within 14 days of completion of item 6
8	Close gaps, document processes, assign ongoing responsibilities, and transfer "ownership"	Close out project assignments	Project manager Project leaders Team members Sub-team members	Complete within 180 days of completion of item 7

Figure 3-5: Project Plan Outline

When you begin to take action according to the project plan, remember that objectives, targets, and goals might need to be changed along the way. If those changes fit within the scope of the project, then by all means accept them and re-strategize on how to accomplish them. If the changes take you completely outside the initial scope, consider re-scoping the project. Use solid project management principles and software; this will help you manage goals and objectives, as well as allow you to share the status of all the phases with your team.

Jack Welch, former CEO of General Electric, had some good advice for this phase: "Once you have the strategy, you execute like hell."

Leading a Successful Project

Creating a corporate university was the most rewarding but difficult project experience I've ever had. It requires extensive planning and a solid business plan, as well as the same work habits and personal characteristics that are needed for success in any major planning or project management effort. Here's what I suggest:

43

- *Have patience.* Remain patient even when things don't seem to go your way. Nothing worth having is ever easy in any business environment. If you have a relatively small amount of patience, I'll guarantee your project will be less effective if even commissioned.

- *Be persistent.* There will be times when things start to lag or look uncertain. Anticipate this, and plan thoroughly. If the project isn't well-thought-out in the first place, hard-headed persistence won't be enough. But if you have a solid business plan, persistence is a strong ally.

- *Work through ambiguity.* Perhaps the most important attribute is to be able to deal with the unknown. Not every piece of the project is wrapped up in a nice package with a bow. The ability to execute short-term goals and set long-term plans that can be changed if necessary is key. Knowing when and how to adjust to change and take advantage of that change will serve you well.

- **Be results-oriented.** Always keep you eye on the ball! Any actions you take must be directly related to the goal. If you are doing things that won't move you forward, you're wasting time.

- **Take charge.** You must be able to make the tough decisions. This does not imply that you get to use marshal law—it simply means that you are responsible to your team and to the project, and that you are supportive of the strategy.

- **Listen.** One thing you must learn how to do is listen. No one has all the answers. You might have the best strategy, but you need people to execute that strategy. Listen to what others are saying, ask them for input, and don't be afraid to give the team "what if" scenarios. You will gain insight into what others think and want, and you will all grow from one another.

- **Collaborate.** Being able to work with other people in the organization is critical to the success of any project. Many times, your personal goals and objectives are not the same as the goals and objectives of individuals and departments who must be involved if you are to get your project off the ground. This is sometimes a bitter pill for people to swallow, but the reality is that collaboration and negotiation is how business gets done—especially in large companies.

- **Benchmark and compare.** Don't reinvent the wheel. Take a look at what others are doing and how they execute their own projects. (The next chapter talks about benchmarking and doing comparative studies.)

Chapter 4

Conducting Benchmarking and Comparisons

Part of the process of creating a corporate university is determining what's already out there that might work well in your organizational culture. One easy way to do that is to conduct benchmarking and comparison studies.

People often get the two confused. *Benchmarking* refers to the process of identifying and determining the best in class: the organization with the best or highest standards, visions, financials, and most importantly, people. Why people? Because people are the common denominator in organizations, and it is their performance that determines standards, visions, financials, and anything else related to business. Find out who has the best sales organization, the most responsive or dedicated customer-service department, the leanest production operation, and the best training and development. Then find out how they do it.

When you start comparing programs or university structures, make sure you're comparing apples to apples, not apples to oranges. Two corporations can have the same programs yet not execute them the same way. Most corporations have succession programs, but some are position-based where others are pool-based. If you're comparing your succession planning program with another corporation, be sure you're comparing apples to apples. Various trade magazines contain a wealth of information about industry leaders and current trends, and how various organizations implement programs and set standards and visions for the future. You need to determine what you have to do to get to where the industry leaders are. Many publications even provide contact information. You'll be surprised at how many people will talk to you about their own experience with the same problems you're having. This will help you visualize the goal and work toward it. You have to figure out what you want to compare first, however, before you do any benchmarking studies.

The key to making comparisons and assessing what is done in other organizations is to look only at those programs that align with your current business strategy.

One corporate university run by a global organization with 24,000 employees had over 240,000 employee hits on its Web site in a one-month period—an average of 100 hits per employee. Let's say your company has 24,000 employees and you experienced only 96,000 hits. Does this mean the other company's university is being used more than yours? Absolutely NOT! The global company might define a "hit" as a link that is clicked or a document that is opened, whereas a hit to you is each time an individual signs in at the university.

Take the time to understand what you're comparing, why you're comparing it, and what benefit it will bring to your organization. Here are some things to consider before you start comparing one corporate university to another.

- *Profit vs. non-profit*
  Ask yourself this question: Are revenues raised through the corporate university? If I'm comparing my university to one that raises revenue, the business model will be completely different and policies affecting the attendees might also be different. That said, I might still want to see offerings within the university, but set them up in a different manner. Financials, however, will be different.

- *Internal university vs. external university*
  Ask yourself this question: Is the university meant only for our employees, or can anyone attend? Internal universities can be easily run on the intranet, whereas external universities use the Internet. Comparing IT factors associated with Internet programs do me no good if my university is internal.

- *Business similarities*
  Ask yourself these questions: What business are we in? What business competencies are we good at? Manufacturing or service? If we're in manufacturing, then comparing universities focusing on service might not be the best approach.

Once the questions have been answered, it's time to quantify the standard, vision, or performance level. That's where comparisons come in to play. Why should you compare? If you don't know what the standard is, you cannot compare against it. The comparison data will tell you what kind of organizations to benchmark.

Once we decide what to benchmark and how to measure it, the key is to collect information about how an organization got to be the best. Figure 4-1 presents an example of a program assessment. In this example, we'll look at what programs organizations place in their corporate universities and how they measure them.

Figure 4-1: Program Assessment

Program Name	Does it currently exist in your organization?		Action		Measurements	Current Profile
	Y	N	Modify	Develop	Metrics	Assessment
Career Development Program site	x		x		• Number of people accessing site • Using as part of Development Plan • Number of high-potentials using site	Need to modify our program. Needs to be included in development planning.
Mentoring	x		x		• Increased retention rates • Job movement within 24 months • Survey program satisfaction results • Performance ratings	Need to modify our program to include job rotation.
First-Line Supervisory Program		x		x	• Number of current managers who attended course . • Managers who have had course and have been promoted	Need to create a program for new managers as seasoned managers leave or retire.
Rotation Program		x			• Performance ratings • Number of people in rotation programs who leave company • Deployment to upper-level management positions within 2 years	Need to create a program for senior managers to increase bench strength in several areas.
Fast-Track Programs		x		x	• Deployment to managerial positions • Deployment to mid-level management positions within 5 years	Need to create a program based on the number of incumbents who will retire.

Common Mistakes in Benchmarking

Benchmarking is embedded in most organizations as part of a competitive strategy. However, there are many opportunities for mistakes in benchmarking. Author Anne Evans listed the ten benchmarking "mistakes" she believes people should avoid:

Mistake #1. Confusing benchmarking with participating in a survey.
A survey of organizations in a similar industry to yours is not benchmarking per se. Such a survey will give you some interesting numbers, but with benchmarking, you learn what is behind the numbers. In other words, a benchmarking survey can tell you where you rank, but it won't help you improve your position (however, it might provide you with some insight as to who to talk with).

Mistake #2. Thinking there are pre-existing "benchmarks" to be found.
Just because some survey or study says that $2.35 is the "benchmark" cost for a particular transaction doesn't mean that you must perform that transaction for that price. The so-called benchmark might not be applicable to your market, customers, or resource levels. Think about your own situation before you use it. Insist on identifying your own benchmarking partners and finding out from them what is achievable, and then decide whether or not you can achieve a similar level of performance.

48

Mistake #3. Forgetting about service delivery and customer satisfaction.
There are plenty of stories about organizations that became so fixated on the costs of providing a product or service that they failed to take the customer into account. Paring down the costs is often followed by a cutback in service, which means that some customers will go elsewhere. This might ultimately cost you your business, so take a "balanced scorecard" approach when developing your benchmarking metrics.

Mistake #4. The process is too large and complex to be manageable.
A process is a group of tasks. A system is a group of processes. Avoid trying to benchmark a total system; it will be extremely costly and time-consuming, and it will be hard to stay focused. Better to select one or several processes in the total system and work with them before moving on to the next part of the system.

Mistake #5. Confusing benchmarking with research.
Benchmarking presupposes that you are working on an existing process for which there is data on its effectiveness and costs. Developing a new employee handbook by collecting other people's handbooks (and taking ideas from them), is research, not benchmarking; it is an entirely new process.

Mistake #6. Misalignment.

"Misalignment" refers to benchmarking something that is not aligned with the overall strategy and goals of the business (or worse, that cuts across some other initiative the organization is already taking). A lead team at the strategic level needs to oversee the benchmarking project and make sure that it is in line with what is happening in the business as a whole.

Mistake #7. Picking a topic that is too intangible and difficult to measure.

"Employee communication" is probably the most slippery concept that exists and is known to be a major problem in so many organizations, but it is a very broad topic. Encourage your benchmarking team to select a part of the topic that can be observed and measured, such as the process of distributing memos to people in the organization.

Mistake #8. Not establishing the baseline.

Some organizations start making benchmarking visits before they have analyzed their own process thoroughly. Benchmarking assumes that you already know your own process and its level of performance. After all, that information is what you have to offer to your benchmarking partners in exchange for the information you are seeking from them. Make sure your benchmarking team is very clear about what it wants to learn before you approach potential benchmarking partners.

Mistake #9. Not researching benchmarking partners thoroughly.

It is essential that you select the right benchmarking partners so that you don't waste their time or yours. One rule in benchmarking etiquette says that you should never ask a benchmarking partner a question that you can answer yourself by researching the literature in the public domain.

Mistake #10. Not having a code of ethics and a contractual agreement with partners.

Your partners should be clear about what you are seeking to learn from them, how that information will be treated, who will have access to it, and for what purposes it will be used. Ideally, this should be formally agreed upon.

49

Chapter 5

Preparing a Strategic Plan

The next step in the process, once you have determined the need for a corporate university and done benchmarking studies, is to develop a strategic plan that documents your strategy and outlines how you will execute it. This chapter will help you develop a strategic plan. Once it is accepted, it should be updated at least semi-annually and incorporated into the business case. I highly recommend the format used here, starting with an executive summary.

Executive Summary

The executive summary should be no longer than two pages. This document is the culmination of the planning stage. It should:

- Align university strategic goals with senior leadership goals and objectives
- Align university goals, performance tasks, and contributions
- Clearly link budget costs, planning, and priorities
- Better manage information for data-driven decision making and predictions
- Outline performance support and rapid deployment of training

If you take each of the bullets above and write a short paragraph on each, explaining how you intend to accomplish these things from what I call the "10,000 foot level," you'll have it. Don't get into detail here—that's what the rest of the strategic plan will do. (Note: It is easier to write the executive summary after you've completed the other sections.)

Values and Operating Concepts

The values and concepts of the corporate university need to align with the corporation's values. Here are values that should be addressed in the strategy if they are important to your organization:

- Customer focus
- Results-driven
- Foster employee participation and development opportunities
- People excellence
- Integrity
- Flexibility
- Accountability
- Technical and managerial competence
- Cost avoidance
- Return on Investment
- Continuous improvement
- Manage by fact
- Safety and environmental awareness

General Products and Services

The strategy can include any or all of these objectives:

- Provide and manage the university for training and development requirements in support of business objectives and goals.
- Facilitate OD and Training functions and intervention strategies.
- Determine training needs and objectives.
- Measure and increase training effectiveness for business units.
- Develop curricula to be used in support of current training and development needs and performance development planning.

- Design, develop, and distribute standardized training, development performance, and support materials that align with business objectives.
- Provide, maintain, and upgrade a Learning Management System for our customers by providing online training opportunities, tracking training curricula, issuing training reports, and managing business unit hierarchies.
- Coordinate learning events and provide accurate information about learning opportunities, times, places, instructors, etc.
- Control and manage financial spending on training and development programs.
- Perform benchmark and comparison studies with outside organizations to bring in best practices as well as training and development implementation strategies.

Key Performance Indicators

You must clearly spell out the relationship between the corporate, business unit, and university functions. Figure 5-1 shows a way to represent alignment.

Figure 5-1: Alignment with Key Performance Indicators

Corporation	Business Unit	University
Customer focus	Customer focus	Provide training and development opportunities
Increase shareholder wealth	Profitable growth	Cost improvements through change in behavior
Integrity	Integrity and ethics	Integrity and ethics training
People excellence	People excellence	University and LMS management
Results-driven	Results-driven	Customer results-driven (metrics)
Safety and environmental awareness	Safety and environmental awareness	Provide safety training
	Financial management	Cost avoidance

53

The next step is to summarize the specific business functions the university will be supporting.

Alignment with the Rest of the Organization

The university must be a supporting function of the organization's business units. Figure 5-2 outlines the alignment of an organization's goals and objectives. How do you plan to increase market share, increase sales without relying on price increases (those only work so long), decrease expenses, outsource SG & A, and so on? All these things are based on your goals and objectives.

What directly impacts the goals and objectives? There are four elements to the equation:

1. Leadership and management
2. Systems and processes
3. Job design
4. Long-term organizational change

Each of the elements supports several business objectives and programs. Some objectives and programs can be supported by more than one element; the key is for you to align the programs with the element.

Figure 5-2: University Alignment

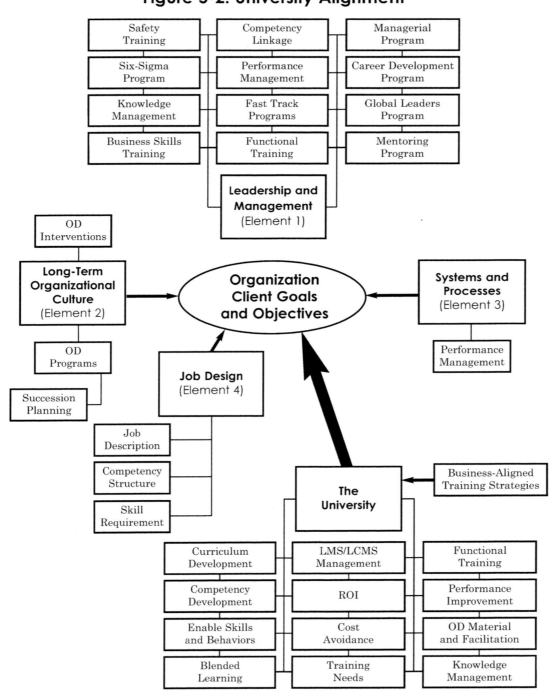

Let's take a closer look at each of the elements: leadership and management, long-term organization culture change, systems and processes, and job design.

Leadership and Management

- *Mentoring Program.* Mentoring is extremely important in today's business climate as a way of developing succession and resource-pool candidates. An organization's mentoring program should be connected in some way to the university, but do not place the entire program in the university. Your strategic plan should explain what the program is, who the intended audience is, and who serves as a point of contact. If you don't have safeguards, everyone will attempt to become a mentor, and if you don't try to regulate this program, you will create a free for all.

  There are some excellent internal and supplier mentoring programs out there. Find out what other organizations are doing regarding these programs and what they want to get from them.

- *Knowledge Management.* Knowledge management all boils down to one thing: Capturing the untapped knowledge that an organization has and applies to its daily operations. To do that, start by creating a link in the university that captures the more common practices by the business units. Once management sees the processes, directives, business cases, comparison studies, metrics, alignments, and standard operating procedures, they can provide direction.

- *Safety Programs.* All business organizations ought to measure safety and build it into every process. Everyone—from the custodian cleaning the bathrooms to the CEO—should be able to create a process that measures whether or not safety is in any way being compromised. The leaders have to instill that in their people. If the leaders care about safety, why should anyone else?

- *Six Sigma.* If you want Six Sigma to be successful, you have to understand two things: First, it's a methodology—not a program. Second, you have to be able to identify what a Six-Sigma project is, what "workouts" are, and what re-engineering is. You can mess up a good thing with Six Sigma if you don't have the right players involved who can see the bigger picture. The key is to "share" experiences, show examples, provide templates, and work with senior leadership. Learning about Six Sigma is one thing; applying it to get business results and sharing the "hows" is something else. Leverage the university to do those things and you will have a strong buy-in to the Six-Sigma methodology, because it *does* work.

- **Fast-Track Programs.** A section of the university should be dedicated to fast-track programs. These programs are normally designed to quickly close a program gap; they normally don't continue on for an extended period of time. (If they do, then they are not fast-track, but instead are "normal" programs.) The idea behind giving them a dedicated place in the university (call it a campus) is that you want fast-track students to be able to put their hands on information quickly. Having a campus creates an intangible feeling of "specialness" and a sense of belonging to the university, thereby strengthening the alignment of the business units and the university in the eyes of senior leadership.

- **Competency Linkage.** Some people believe that competency models are ambiguous, but keep in mind that the university must have a set of competencies aligned to training and development opportunities. Competencies build the framework within which people can work, learn, and grow. For example, let's take a competency like conflict resolution, which focuses on dealing with and resolving conflict within a team. You should provide leaders and managers with a list of training courses and learning opportunities that will help an individual develop that competency. This could include courses in conflict management and how to lead a cross-functional team on a high-visibility project. You could take the development a step further by having the individual brief the CFO or CEO, if the project warrants it.

- **Business Skills Training.** This type of training focuses on improving management skills (i.e., leading teams, performance management, interpersonal skills, financial training, mergers, acquisitions, etc.). The common error people make regarding training opportunities is that the skills are not used quickly enough by the participant (if at all). I can go to a financial institution and learn all I need to learn about mergers and acquisitions, but if I wait a year before I use it, I'm sure to forget many things. A university should provide the needed business skills for the organization's business units *when they need them*. Conduct a thorough needs assessment and you should be able to identify which business skills are key.

- *Career Development.* This should include self-assessments of various types that help an individual identify their strengths, weaknesses, and opportunities in the organization. You should have some sort of link to a document or database that identifies internal job opportunities. Some corporate universities display career ladders along with career stoppers or stallers associated with positions they are currently in and tips on how to avoid them.

- *Global Leaders Programs.* If your corporation is global, it's wise to provide only information: an introduction to what the program is, who the intended audience is, and a point of contact.

- *Technical/Functional Skills.* The technical and functional skills associated with any position should be linked to curricula positioned in a Learning Management System (LMS). A link from the university to an LMS is best.

- *Performance Management.* The university's Strategic Plan should also cover or include the performance management policy, associated forms, points of contact, and the best examples of completed forms that help people walk through the process. Step-by-step job aids work very well.

The Strategic Plan must contain an explanation of the program, why it exists, what the expectations are, as well as the benefits it brings to the corporation and the people. Former head of General Electric, Jack Welch, said in his book *Winning,* "Companies win when their managers make a clear and meaningful distinction between top- and bottom-performing businesses and people, when they cultivate the strong and cull the weak. Companies suffer when every business and person is treated equally and bets are sprinkled all around like rain on the ocean."[5]

- *Managers' Program.* This first-line supervisory program should be made up of HR programs for managers, online coaching, and job aids. The university should be leveraged to provide information, training, and learning events prior to anyone taking on the role of manager. Many corporations fail to do this.

Why would a corporation promote people into management without even providing them a hint of how they should execute to meet the requirements of the job?

Long-Term Culture Change

- *OD Programs.* As I explained earlier, partnering with OD is critical. The university can become a solid tool to house personality assessment data, leadership and climate surveys, and measuring competencies. If this type of information is to be collected into a university, however, it must be and remain confidential. To do this, you need to pass on the information to a Human Resource Information System.

- *OD Interventions.* Incorporating OD intervention actions into the university is a great way to share and learn as well as identify next steps. I'll share an OD intervention regarding sales and the university. While I was working with an outside client, the client mentioned that all the various sales regions have their own ideas of what a training curriculum should look like for salespeople. She went on to say some regions use a variety of training suppliers, one region develops their own training, and another uses one specific supplier for all training. I asked if they are selling different products in the regions. "No," she said. I asked what they think they need versus what they really need. She said, "The regional managers have identified what the salespeople need in the way of training." I asked what the salespeople think they need. She said, "Not what the managers think."

This is a classic and common problem: The managers know everything, but the employees who are actually doing the job don't. This could very well be the problem, therefore we assembled two surveys: one for the sales managers and the other for the salespeople. We launched the surveys from a sales campus in the university. Once we tallied the results and sat down with the managers and employees, it was easy to work out a sales training curriculum complete with developmental assignments as they related to each sales region. We still had a problem in terms of what internal training to develop versus what was available from a supplier.

As the meeting to debate/decide which supplier to use continued, I asked these questions: Which supplier tells us the best way to sell our products? What supplier tells us how to close the sale? What supplier tells us the best way our products help organizations in their applications? The room was quiet.

Someone said, "None of them do that." I said, maybe we should think about that. We developed a template that identified the product, its application, the customers who use this product and what they use it for, questions to

59

ask, and techniques to close the sale. Again, I don't like re-inventing the wheel, but we needed four fresh tires to get back in the race. This information along with how salespeople learn it is now in the sales campus in their university, and the sales teams are responsible for its upkeep. It allows a salesperson to understand what the products are, who uses them, what they use them for, and the benefits the customer gets from them. This insight helps execute the achievement of sales and customer understanding. This gives you an idea of things you can place in the university. The possibilities are endless.

Job Design

- *Job Description and Skill Requirements.* As you try to determine what training and development support will be needed for a position, don't do what some organizations do—fail to include job descriptions and skill requirements. When written correctly, job descriptions provide insight and information about the general function of a job (technical) and which business units/products/programs each job supports. The skill requirements identify the minimum acceptable tasks the individual is expected to perform. Job descriptions are and will continue to be somewhat ambiguous, but for the designer and developer of the corporate university, identifying skill requirements and understanding how the position fits into the corporation provides insight as to what training and development courses and programs need to be developed or included.

- *Competency Structure.* A core competency is the fundamental knowledge, ability, or expertise in a specific subject area or skill set, such as engineering, data storage, purchasing, investing, accounting applications, etc.

Necessary Competencies

A corporation normally requires specific competencies according to where they fit in line and staff functions. Figure 5-3 illustrates a simple yet effective way to align competencies to learning requirements.

Figure 5-3: Competency to Learning Requirement

Front-Line Employees (example of necessary competencies)			
Competency	Related Learning Requirement	Platform	Supplier
Business Acumen	Understanding Business	Choose type of learning platform for each learning requirement. Platforms could be classroom, OJT, e-learning, seminars, symposiums, learning groups, self-study, etc.	Supplier name or "internal"
Business Acumen	Principles of Marketing		
Business Acumen	Business Finance		
Time Management	Setting Priorities at Work		
Action-Oriented	Taking Initiative		
Action-Oriented	Improving Your Productivity		
Action-Oriented	Interpersonal Skills		
Results-Driven	Creating Strategic Partnerships		
Results-Driven	Problem-Solving Fundamentals		
Communication	Presentation Skills		
Communication	Communicating Effectively		
Ethics and Integrity	Business Ethics		
Integrity and Trust	Building Trust in Teams and the Workplace		

(continued)

61

Figure 5-3: Competency to Learning Requirement *(continued)*

Manager (example of necessary competencies)			
Competency	**Related Learning Requirement**	**Platform**	**Supplier**
Management of Processes	How to Effectively Plan and Organize	Choose type of learning platform for each learning requirement. Platforms could be classroom, OJT, e-learning, seminars, symposiums, learning groups, self-study, etc.	Supplier name or "internal"
Management of Processes	How to Manage Information		
Customer Focus	Effective Communication		
Customer Focus	Interaction Skills with Subordinates		
Managing Diversity	How to Value Differences		
Managing Diversity	Interaction Skills with Subordinates		
Managing Diversity	Communicating with Others		
Delegation	Using Delegating		
Developing and Directing People	Performance Management		
Developing and Directing People	Development of Others		
Developing and Directing People	Preparing People to Succeed		
Developing and Directing People	Coaching Basics		
Developing and Directing People	Facilitating Improved Performance		
Developing and Directing People	Listening Skills		
Developing and Directing People	Communicating and Listening		
Developing and Directing People	Building Effective Teams		
Command Skills	Adapting to Changing Environments		
Command Skills	Personal Empowerment		
Command Skills	Taking Action to Solve Problems		
Conflict Management	Conflict Resolution Processes		
Conflict Management	Resolving Team Conflict		
Conflict Management	Solving Work Conflicts		
Conflict Management	How to Manage Difficult People		

(continued)

Figure 5-3: Competency to Learning Requirement *(concluded)*

Director (example of necessary competencies)			
Competencies (In addition to all managerial competencies)	**Related Training Courses or Information**	**Training Course Supplier**	**Contact Information**
Hiring and Staffing	Screening Resumes and Interviewing Skills	Choose type of learning platform for each learning requirement. Platforms could be classroom, OJT, e-learning, seminars, symposiums, learning groups, self-study, etc.	Supplier name or "internal"
Motivating Others	Influencing Others		
	Interaction Skills		
Building Effective Teams	Creating High Performance Teams		
	Negotiating Skills		
	Leading Teams		
	Inspiring Leadership Commitment		
Managing Vision and Purpose	Facilitating Change in the Organization		
	Adapting to Change		
	Helping Managers Adapt to Change		
Organizational Agility	Aligning Performance Strategy with Business Strategy		
	Aligning Organizational Capability		

Financial Analysis

Figure 5-4 shows how to present financial analysis that provides initial costs associated with the university concept.

Figure 5-4: High Level Financial Analysis (example)

Expense Category	2003	2004	2005	2006	2007 NPV	2008 NPV	2009 NPV
Learning Management System							
LMS online	$75,000	–	–	–	–	–	–
Automatic flow events	–	–	$13,000	–	–	–	–
Testing software	$6,400	–	–	–	–	–	–
On-site support	$2,500	$2,000	$5,000	$0	$0	$0	$0
Licensing	$10,400	–	–	–	–	–	–
Maintenance costs	–	$12,220	$0	$0	$0	$0	$0
Subtotal LMS	$94,300	$14,220	$18,000	$0	$0	$0	$0
Hardware							
Servers	$7,500	–	–	–	–	–	–
Subtotal Hardware	$7,500	–	–	–	–	–	–
Marketing							
Advertising (online)	–	–	$0	$0	$0	$0	$0
Printed brochures	–	–	$500	$100	$0	$0	$0
Brochures (online)	–	–		$0	$0	$0	$0
Subtotal Marketing	–	–	$500	$100	$0	$0	$0
Online Vendor Programs							
Online softskills	$32,000	$32,000	$36,000	$38,900	$35,000	$35,000	$35,000
Online coaching	–	–	$5,000	$0	$0	$0	$0
Subtotal Online Vendor	$32,000	$32,000	$41,000	$38,900	$35,000	$35,000	$35,000
Labor (ABC Costing)							
University design/maintenance	–	$2,000	$8,000	$20,000	$30,000	$30,000	$30,000
LMS upgrades/inputs	$8,000	$8,000	$8,000	$6,000	$4,000	$3,000	$3,000
Consultant fees	–	–	$0	$0	$0	$0	$0
Subtotal Labor	$8,000	$10,000	$16,000	$26,000	$34,000	$33,000	$33,000
ANNUAL EXPENDITURES	$141,800	$56,220	$75,500	$65,000	$69,000	$68,000	$68,000

Expenditures for a seven-year period amount to $544,510 (less than .0002 of $3 billion in sales). On-site support by the LMS provider, as well as vendor training programs, comes from the business unit, not the university (unless the university is designed to generate revenue). The university aids the business unit in selection of the vendor and places information about it in the LMS, including links to obtain training.

Customer Identification

Figure 5-5 shows how to list the internal customers (IC) and the external customers (EC) for the university. Some corporations list subsidiaries as external customers if they operate autonomously. It's your decision how you label customers.

Figure 5-5: Customer Identification and Code Assignments (example)

Customers			
Code	Internal Customer Group	Code	External Customer Group
IC1	Business A Operations (USA)	EC1	Subsidiary X
IC2	Business B Operations (USA)	EC2	Subsidiary Y
IC3	Business C Operations (Europe)	EC3	Subsidiary Z
IC4	Operations Management		
IC5	Sales (USA)		
IC6	Sales (Europe)		
IC7	Sales Management		
IC8	Logistics		
IC9	IT		
IC10	Procurement		
IC11	Quality Assurance		
IC12	Six Sigma		
IC13	Safety		
IC14	Finance		
IC15	Human Resources		
IC16	Distribution		
IC17	University		

Suppliers and Services

Figure 5-6 shows how to list suppliers for the university.

Figure 5-6: Suppliers and Services (example)

Suppliers					
Code	Internal Supplier	Service Provided	Code	External Supplier	Service Provided
IS1	Corporate communication	University Web page design and management	ES1		Sales classroom training
IS2	IT	Program applications	ES2		Soft and business skills classroom training
IS3	Technical communication	Instructor-led course materials repository	ES3		Learning Management System
			ES4		Leadership Development classroom courses
			ES5		Soft skills classroom training and coaching via Web
			ES6		Video and DVD creation
			ES7		Project Management classroom training
			ES8		Technical self-study training
			ES9		Sales classroom training
			ES10		Soft and business skills training via Web

Requirements for Customer Support

Figure 5-7 shows how to document the products and services provided using a customer code. It also identifies the requirement for customer support, how you will measure against that requirement, and the expected performance level.

Figure 5-7: Current Customer Support Requirements (example)

Customer Code	Product or Service	Customer Support Requirement	Quality Indicator (to include metrics)	Expected Performance Level
IC1 to IC17	Provide and manage the university for training and development requirements in support of business objectives and goals	Access university through intranet and Internet to obtain training and development opportunities	University visits, page views, and site hits	University can be accessed 24 hours per day via company and personal computers
IC4, IC7, IC12, IC16	Facilitate OD function and intervention strategies	Provide OD in leadership/ management, systems and processes, job design, and organization culture change	Overall customer satisfaction, ROI	Provide and help implement the alternatives to solve customer problems
IC1 to IC17	Determine training needs and objectives	Properly identify training needs as skill-driven, attitude-driven, or competency-driven	Completed training planner forms	Differentiate training needs versus OD interventions or other non-training intervention
IC1 to IC17	Measure and increase training effectiveness for business units	Provide documentation that measures the effectiveness of the training solution	Overall training effectiveness levels that reach a minimum of 3.0 on 4-point Likert scale	Maintain a minimum of 3.0 across the enterprise
IC1 to IC17	Develop curricula to be used in support of current training and development needs and performance development planning	Design and apply curricula that include New Hire, Safety, Functional and Technical, Interpersonal Skills, and Leadership	All participants in the LMS have curricula attached to their record	All curricula show as either in-work or complete

67

(continued)

Figure 5-7: Current Customer Support Requirements (example)
(concluded)

Customer Code	Product or Service	Customer Support Requirement	Quality Indicator (to include metrics)	Expected Performance Level
IC1 to IC17, EC1, EC2, EC3	Design, develop, and issue standardized training and development perform-ance support materials that align with business objectives	Provide accurate and technically correct training materials that meet quality and usability requirements	Overall customer satisfaction	Customer satisfaction levels are at least a "MET" on the scale
IC1 to IC17, EC1	Provide, maintain, and upgrade Learning Management System for our customers by providing online training opportunities, tracking training curricula, providing training reports, and managing business unit hierarchies	Provide training information in accessible, easy-to-read, effective, and understandable online formats, with testing and the ability to increase performance capability. View the LMS for pertinent training and develop-ment information on employees	Completed self-study courses, completed instructor-led courses, total training hours per employee, and LMS visits	LMS is the preferred system and process to track, record, and provide online training course and classroom information
IC1 to IC17, EC1, EC2	Coordinate training events and provide accurate information about training opportunities, times, places, instructors, etc.	Be made aware of the training opportunities available throughout	Completed self-study courses, completed instructor-led courses, total training hours per employee, and LMS visits	All employees know how to use the university and LMS
IC1 to IC17, EC1, EC2	Control and management of financial spending on training programs	Make sure customers aren't spending dollars on supplier courses and opportunities we have in-house or have with approved third-party suppliers (cost avoidance)	Cost-avoidance dollars	Identify cost-avoidance dollars to the customer
IC17	Benchmark and comparison studies with outside organizations to bring in best practices, as well as training and development implementation strategies	Apply best practice and benchmark studies to our current training and development strategies	Overall customer satisfaction	Attend at least one conference per year, and perform benchmarking and comparison studies to other companies

Critical Future Requirements

Figure 5-8 lists the requirements of the customer in our example for the short and longer term.

Figure 5-8: Future Requirements (example)

Customer Code	Requirements	Expected Performance Level	Project Plan	Metrics
IC1–IC5	Curricula for all employees and OD interventions, and access to LMS and campuses in university	Provide the same training and development opportunities as the U.S. and Canada	Yes	Use the same metrics as the U.S. and Europe
IC1	Simulation programs to drive operational efficiency	Access to a simulation program that pinpoints efficiency	In-work	Cost avoidance as a result of using the program and/or ROI
IC3	Complete training and development system	System can be used in the U.S. and Europe	Yes	Use the same metrics as U.S.
IC11	Develop quality assurance (QA) materials	Employees complete all QA training online	Yes	Cost avoidance associated with online versus classroom training

Current Requirements for Suppliers

Figure 5-9 shows how to list specific requirements of an identified supplier. These statements in the "Our Requirement" column should contain a brief explanation of the requirement. The Performance Indicator is the minimum requirement for acceptable performance from the supplier.

Figure 5-9: Supplier Requirements (example)

Supplier Code	Our Requirement	Performance Indicator
IS1	Maintain ability to access university and enable Web page development	95% availability rate
IS2	Access to program applications	98% availability rate
IS3	Provide reliability to access approved course materials and reproduce when required	98% availability rate
ES1	Provide information about sales training courses and provide us with a report of courses attended by employees	98% satisfaction rate
ES2	Provide information about upcoming vendor courses and provide us with a report of courses attended by employees	98% satisfaction rate
ES3	Provide updated releases for LMS software, provide telephone support, provide product specialization	100% satisfaction rate
ES4	Provide information about upcoming managerial courses and provide us with a report of courses attended by employees	100% satisfaction rate
ES5	Provide access and introduce instructors to new concepts and support materials	100% satisfaction rate
ES6	Provide video production and DVD support of training projects	100% satisfaction rate
ES7	Train employees in project management and provide us with a report of courses	100% satisfaction rate
ES9	Provide information about sales training courses and provide us with a report of courses attended by employees	100% satisfaction rate
ES10	Provide a library of online soft skills and business skills in training modules that work with our LMS	100% satisfaction rate

Future Products and Services (within 2 years)

Figure 5-10 shows how to list future products and services for the selected customer code. You should verify this to make sure you list all of the corporation's products and services, as well as those that are expected to come online within the next two years.

Figure 5-10: Future Products and Services (examples)

Product or Service	Customer Code
Workout (KAIZEN) Facilitators	IC1–IC24
Increase the number of campuses in the university	IC3, IC5, IC8, IC11, IC12, IC16, IC17
Create First-Line Supervisory Program	IC1–IC24
Create Knowledge Management Centers for business clients	IC1–IC24

KPI Breakout

Figure 5-11 presents a Key Performance Indicator (KPI) breakout that aligns the KPI, key processes, critical success factors, and the current capability to achieve the KPI. The first column, KPI, uses the same statements used in the Key Performance Indicator Alignment section (this has already been presented). Statements in the second column, Key Process, are the same statements taken from the Current Customer Support Requirements table. The Critical Success Factors (CSFs) in column three are the tools/skills required to achieve the Key Process. The last column shows current capability or current assessment of how well the company uses those tools/skills. (You and the staff must perform a self-assessment of each CSF.)

Use a simple red, yellow, and green color box to indicate the current capability where:

- Red (R) represents a tool/skill that cannot be used or achieved more than 75 percent of the time.
- Yellow (Y) represents a tool/skill that can be used or achieved between 76 percent and 90 percent of the time.
- Green (G) represents a tool/skill that cannot be used or achieved more than 91 percent of the time.

These percentages are somewhat subjective, but they do help determine which areas need prompt attention, which ones need tweaking, and which ones are running effectively.

Figure 5-11: KPI Alignment (example)

KPI	Key Process	Critical Success Factor (CSF)	Current Capability
Provide Training and Development Opportunities/ Improvements	Determine training needs and objectives	Use training planners	G
		Use needs-assessment forms	G
		Use Employee Skills Inventory program sheet	Y
	Design, develop, and distribute standardized training and development performance-support materials that align with business objectives	Use ISD approach	G
		Utilize material designer for all internally developed training products	G
	Develop curricula to be used in support of current training and development needs	Use training planner/assessment to develop draft curricula	G
		Use employee skills inventories	G
		Draft curriculum approved by management	Y
		Work with safety managers on safety curricula	Y
		Place approved curricula in LMS	Y
		Assign employees to training curricula	G
	Coordinate training events and provide accurate information about training opportunities, times, places, instructors, etc.	Coordinate with LMS Administrator	R
		Procure instructors and make sure TTT is complete	G
		Use LMS to mark courses attended	G

(continued)

Figure 5-11: KPI Alignment (example)
(continued)

KPI	Key Process	Critical Success Factor (CSF)	Current Capability
University and LMS Management	Determine training needs and objectives	Make sure only valid training needs are placed in the LMS	G
		Make sure non-training needs requiring job aids are in university	Y
	Measure and increase training effectiveness for business units	Use LMS e-mail flows to send survey form 90 to 120 days after a participant completes a course	R
	Develop curricula to be used in support of current training and development needs and performance development planning (Performance Development)	Seamless portal from university to the LMS	Y
		Link to view the Employee Skills Inventory	G
		Link for the curriculum assignment process	G
		Link in the HR Center of how to write a development plan	G
	Provide, maintain, and upgrade LMS for our customers by providing online training opportunities, tracking training curricula, providing training reports, and managing business unit hierarchies	Successfully manage vendor relationships and pricing options	G
		Install LMS upgrades to the server	G
		Make sure reporting hierarchies are kept up with, using payroll information	G
		Develop standardized reports in the LMS vs. individual reports	Y
		Confirm proper functioning of self-study software to automatically update training records	Y
		Make sure training rosters are sent for input	G
		Procure required IT support for system troubleshooting	G
	Perform benchmark and comparison studies with outside organizations to bring in best practices as well as training and development implementation strategies	Perform benchmarking and comparison studies with similar organizations	G
		Attend conferences and expositions to determine which trends are worth looking into	Y
		Keep up with current training and development trends in the industry	G

73

(continued)

Figure 5-11: KPI Alignment (example)
(concluded)

KPI	Key Process	Critical Success Factor (CSF)	Current Capability
Customer Results-Driven	Measure and increase training effectiveness for business units	"Metrics Dashboard" that provides measurement data (see next section of text)	G
		Measure cost-avoidance dollars for client	G
Cost Avoidance	Measure and increase training effectiveness for business units	Measure cost-avoidance dollars for client	G
		ROI calculations	R
	Control and manage financial spending on training programs	Obtain approval to purchase a vendor course must come from our group to ensure smart spending	G
Cost Improvements through Behavior Change	Facilitate OD function and intervention strategies	Measure and increase training effectiveness for business units	Y
		Project Management Skills to manage intervention	Y
Integrity and Ethics	Design, develop, and distribute standardized training and development performance support materials that align with business objectives	Make sure materials are not copies of copyrighted materials	G
		Make sure links in university and the LMS are authorized and approved by CEO	G

Organizational Gaps

Figure 5-12 shows how to identify critical success factors that are less than desirable yellow or red (in our case—see example below) and the action plans to get them to green.

Figure 5-12: Organization Gaps (example)

KPI	Key Process	Critical Success Factor	Action Plan
University and LMS Management	Measure and increase training effectiveness for business units	Use LMS to send survey form 90 to 120 days after a participant completes a course	Make arrangements for employees' surveys to be sent automatically 90 to 120 days after completion of training
	Develop curricula to be used in support of current training and development needs and performance development planning	Link in the university HR center on how to develop a Performance Development Plan	Need HR approval to place this in the university
	Provide, maintain, and upgrade LMS for our customers by providing online training opportunities, tracking training curricula, providing training reports, and managing business unit hierarchies	Develop standardized reports in the LMS vs. individual reports	Create reports that managers can choose from in LMS
		Make sure classroom training rosters are sent for input	Standardized rosters are available in the university. All training rosters should have fax numbers on them
		Procure required IT support for system troubleshooting	If the university continues at its current pace, might need to procure an IT support person
Cost Avoidance	Measure and increase training effectiveness for business units	ROI calculations	Computer ROI calculations on technical instructor-led courses
	Control and manage financial spending on training programs.	Obtain approval to purchase a vendor course from group to ensure smart spending	This will have to be agreed upon by senior leadership; partner with procurement
Cost Improvement through Behavior Change	Facilitate OD function and intervention strategies	Measure and increase training effectiveness for business units	Utilize forms in Knowledge Management to collect data

SWOT Analysis

The SWOT Analysis shown below presents a way for the university to assess current capabilities and determine future organizational requirements to reach goals and objectives. This analysis shows whether or not the organization has the resources required to reach an objective, and whether or not it needs to find another means of accomplishing its objectives.

Figure 5-13: SWOT Analysis (example)

Key Processes	Strengths	Weaknesses	Opportunities	Threats
Determine training needs and objectives	Use standardized training planner to help determine training needs (versus some other type of intervention)	Not all training courses have a completed planner	Business unit management needs analysis forms to identify possible training needs	Competition
Design, develop, and distribute standardized training and development performance support materials that align with business objectives	Employees are in place to perform and manage	Not all current training courses have a completed planner		Competition
Develop curricula to be used in support of current training and development needs and performance development planning	Curricula are available or are being developed and attached to employees in LMS Employee inventories are being used to aid the development process	Performance development not being used by the manager No follow-up to determine whether or not training courses being selected are based on performance development		Competition

(continued)

Figure 5-13: SWOT Analysis (example)
(concluded)

Key Processes	Strengths	Weaknesses	Opportunities	Threats
Coordinate training events and provide accurate information about training opportunities, times, places, instructors, etc.	Business unit trainers have access in the LMS to schedule courses		Identify training points of contact at each facility	Competition
Measure and increase training effectiveness for business units	"Metrics Dashboard" (see next section) Alignment with business goals and objectives through a strategic plan		Share cost avoidance with senior management	Competition
Perform benchmark and comparison studies with outside organizations to bring in best practices, as well as training and development implementation strategies	Benchmarked, conducted, and documented comparison studies of the top 100 training companies in the U.S. and Canada		Compete in top-100 training companies competition	Competition
Control and manage financial spending on training programs	Compute cost avoidance of business and courses in business and soft skills	(We do not have any inputs as to what businesses can spend on outside vendor or supplier training programs.)		Competition
Facilitate OD function and intervention strategies	Have engaged in OD interventions in leadership and management, systems and processes, job design and organizational change		To perform more of this service and help determine and uncover training and development needs	

77

A Strategic Plan associated with action plans should apply across a wide spectrum of business institutions, regardless of the size of the organization or whether it is public or private.

Metrics Dashboards

A *metrics dashboard* is a self-coined term used to refer to an illustration of the Key University Performance Indicators in a single glance—a one-page document that helps determine the health of the university. The specific goals and objectives of the university and how they are tied to executables for the organization determine what should be on the "dashboard." Each metric on the dashboard should be supported by other metrics.

Here is how it works: Let's say your company sets up a corporate university as a revenue generator. Obviously, one of the key performance metrics is the amount of revenue generated. This would clearly be on the dashboards of the chief learning officer (CLO), chief operating officer (COO), and maybe the chief executive officer (CEO) to view. Figure 5-14 illustrates the revenues for the past eight quarters (two years). The measurements are based on the number of people from other corporations, businesses, and institutions who attend the courses. The offerings are normally instructor-led courses. For the purposes of providing and distinguishing examples, we'll presume that courses for the revenue generation are instructor-led.

Figure 5-14: University Revenues

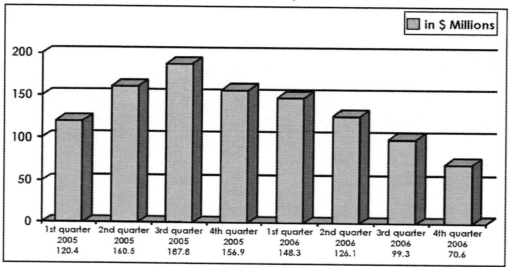

	1st quarter 2005	2nd quarter 2005	3rd quarter 2005	4th quarter 2005	1st quarter 2006	2nd quarter 2006	3rd quarter 2006	4th quarter 2006
in $ Millions	120.4	160.5	187.8	156.9	148.3	126.1	99.3	70.6

In Figure 5-14, we see that revenue has dropped from $187.8 million in the third quarter of 2005 to $70.6 million in the fourth quarter of 2006—a decrease of 62 percent. Supporting metrics to the key performance metric of revenue generation could be:

- Revenue by course offerings
- Number of courses offered
- Types of courses offered (e.g., Financial, Managerial, Leadership, Human Resources, and Computer and revenues for each). The metric is dependent on what strategies and goals you're aligning to.

These could be separate metrics or combinations. Figure 5-15 shows revenues for a strategic managerial course compared to the number of courses offered over the past eight quarters.

Figure 5-15: Revenue to Specific Course Offering (Strategic Management)

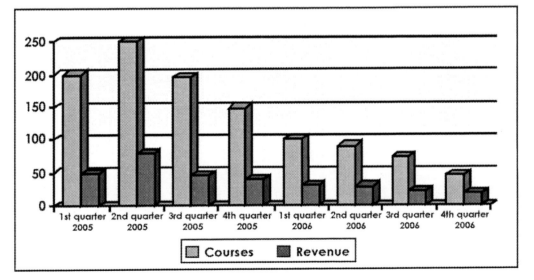

Figure 5-16 illustrates how to present the number of course type offerings over the past eight quarters. Figure 5-17 shows how to present the revenue amount by course type.

Figure 5-16: Course Offerings (by type)

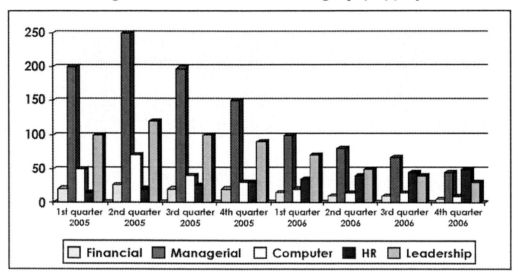

Figure 5-17: Revenue or Course Offerings (by type)

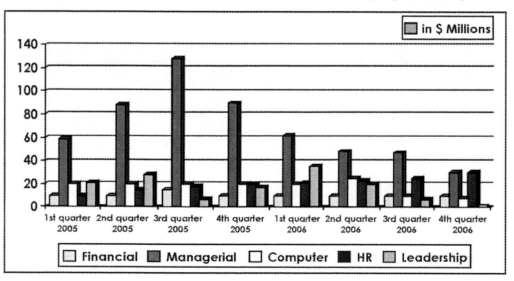

Another key performance metric will be Operating Profit. Figure 5-18 illustrates how to show revenue generation compared to Operating Profit (OP).

Figure 5-18: Total Revenues (compared to OP)

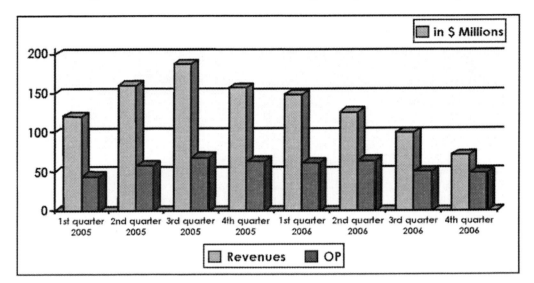

Supporting metrics to the key performance metric of Total Revenues to OP could be:

81

- Revenues by course offerings compared to OP
- Revenues by course type compared to OP

Figure 5-19 presents one way of listing additional measures if your university is to be a revenue generator. A corporate university that is set up to be a revenue generator for the corporation normally uses Level I and Level II measurement metrics, because leaders are more interested in short-term financial results than longer-term behavioral changes. If the university is not set up to be a revenue generator, the focus might instead be on behavioral change.

Figure 5-19: Metrics Dashboard for Revenue Generation University (example)

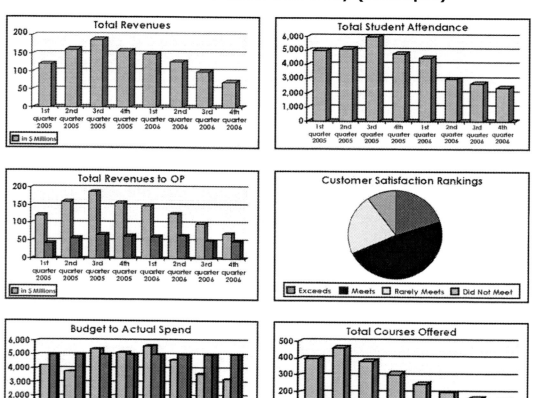

Figure 5-20 illustrates possible key performance metrics to be placed on the dashboard if the university is not a revenue generator. The university, likely accessed via Internet or intranet, would focus on behavioral change. Training and performance curricula would be based on needs assessment and business-unit goals, objectives, and task requirements in the form of curricula in the Learning Management System. Level I through Level IV measurements and supporting metrics should appear on this dashboard.

Figure 5-20: Metrics to Include on a Dashboard (example)

Key Metric on Dashboard	Supporting Metrics/Measurements
Total student attendance	• Total students attending instructor-led courses • Total students attending/completing online courses • Total students attending/completing certification, seminars, etc.
Students completing assigned curricula	• Curricula completed by business unit
Number of times university was accessed	• Total students accessing the university • Web pages visited most often • Average visit time
Behavioral changes/Program effectiveness	• Based on courses (technical or managerial) • Based on course completion • Time to complete course • Course completion compared to increased performance • Course completion compared to high potential candidacy • Course completion compared to promotion
Cost avoidance	• Cost of attending internal courses versus external courses
LMS effectiveness	• Number of times the LMS was accessed by students • Up-time the university was available for students
Customer satisfaction rates (typically Levels I and II)	• Surveys to assess how well the course was liked and understanding of the process • Would the student use the training materials to help them make decisions?

No matter what kind of key performance metrics you want or need to measure, you must have supporting metrics. Some will be important enough to place on the metrics dashboard.

83

Chapter 6

Training and Learning Platforms

If you are setting up a corporate university, you will have a variety of learning and training platforms to choose from. Select platforms that provide the most effective application of skills to associated performance levels. Corporations vary in their IT infrastructure (from dial-up to wireless); the point is to use the training and learning platforms with the lowest bandwidth if your system has low bandwidth. Always keep your IT people involved in planning or upgrading training via the Web. There are many new software products on the market that support effective training and development; however, they won't all work with current infrastructures. For example, employees who need to access training documents residing on the university system or an LMS via a dial-up modem will not be able to open up documents greater than, say, 300KB, so plan accordingly.

Figure 6-1 illustrates training and learning platform approaches and normal bandwidth requirements.

Figure 6-1: Training and Learning Platforms

Training Platform	Best used when	Support Products	Assessment Type	Average Required Bandwidth
Written document formats	Disseminating basic information (awareness) about a process, program, or procedure	• Adobe • Word documents • PowerPoint • Excel	• Written testing • Self-directed exercises • Written scenarios	Low (provided the document size isn't too large)
Structured on-the-job (OJT)	Task is to be demonstrated or performed by a trainee and evaluated by trained staff	OJT checklists	Performance criteria (go or no-go)	Low (provided the document size isn't too large)
Computer-based (CD-ROM) programs	Disseminating basic information (awareness) about a process, program, or procedure that won't often change	Various software	• Self-directed exercises • Simulations in the program • Questions in the program	Medium, depending on software used
Web-based (e-learning)	Disseminating basic or advanced information about a process, program, or procedure that requires some interaction from the trainee	Various software	• Online testing • Self-directed exercises • Simulations	Medium, depending on software used
Instructor-led (classroom)	Disseminating advanced information about a process, program, or procedure that requires interaction and trainee demonstration in a group environment	See above support products	• Self-directed exercises • Simulations • In-class exercises • Performance criterion • Class exercises • Projects • Labs • How-to videos	N/A

Blended learning uses a variety of training platforms and places them into a driven learning style.

- Skill-driven learning, which combines self-paced learning with instructor, supervisor, or facilitator support to develop specific knowledge and skills
- Attitude-driven learning, which mixes various events and delivery media in order to develop specific behaviors
- Competency-driven learning, which blends performance support tools with knowledge management resources and mentoring to develop workplace competencies

Figure 6-2 breaks down these three learning types.

Figure 6-2: Learning Models

Learning Model	Why	How
Skill-driven	Learning specific knowledge and skills requires constant feedback and support from the trainer, supervisor, and peers	• Create a group-learning plan that's self-paced but on a strict schedule • Utilize self-paced/study learning material with instructor-led courses and closing sessions • Demonstrate procedures and processes through synchronous online learning labs • Traditional classroom training • Design long-term projects and follow up with the learning from the outcome
Attitude-driven	Content relevant to developing new attitudes and behaviors requires supervisor-to-trainee and peer-to-peer interactions (preferably in a risk-free environment)	• Hold synchronous Web-based meetings • Assign group projects that are to be completed outside normal work hours or off-site • Conduct role-playing simulations • Use real scenarios with problem-solution outcomes in group or individual sessions
Competency-driven	To capture and transfer tacit knowledge, learners must interact with and observe experts on the job to compare their skills/behaviors to what is required to meet the competency.	• Assign mentors to mentees • Place individuals in development assignments, such as leading a team or project • Assign post-work with periodic reports sent to senior management

87

You should be familiar with various technological and non-technological approaches if you intend to use the skill-driven model. Figures 6-3, 6-4, and 6-5 outline some of these methods.

Figure 6-3: Skill-Driven Technological and Non-technological Approaches

Skill-Driven	Technology Techniques	Non-technology Techniques
Initial communication	• Learning management system • E-mail groups • E-mail leaders and cascade to direct reports • Online university • Instant messaging	• Flyers • Mail drops • Phone messaging • Bulletin boards
Conduct overview session	• E-mail with attached documents • Webinars	• Traditional classroom setting
Self-paced learning	• Web-based • E-books • Online simulations • Commentaries	• Articles to read and comment on • Books or e-books to read and comment on • Job aids • Participant workbooks • Pre-course assignments
Practice	• Simulations with instantaneous feedbacks	• OJT practice with mentor or coach • Related assignments
Demonstration	• Simulations (synchronous with group is best for skill-driven approach) • Asynchronous	• Classroom • OJT with mentor or coach
Feedback	• E-mail • Online survey	• One-on-one coaching • Printed survey
Qualification	• Online testing • Online simulations with go and no-go feedback	• Printed test • Classroom qualification and presentation

88

Figure 6-4: Attitude-Driven Technological and Non-technological Approaches

Attitude-Driven	Technology Techniques	Non-technology Techniques
Initial communication	• Learning management system • E-mail groups • E-mail leaders and cascade to direct reports • Online university • Instant messaging	• Flyers • Mail drops • Phone messaging • Bulletin boards
Conduct overview session	• E-mail with attached document • Webinar	• Traditional classroom
Self-paced learning	• Web-based tutorials • E-books • Simulations	• Read related articles • Read related books • Job aids • Complete workbooks and deploy as pre-work toward classroom training
Practice	• Simulations with real scenarios • Web-based testing	• Group project environments (peer-to-peer)
Demonstration	• Synchronous (online)	• OJT with mentor or coach
Feedback	• Webinars • Chat rooms • Online survey • Online 360° assessments	• Role playing with peers • Formal feedback with coaching
Qualification	• Synchronous (online)	• Classroom qualification exams and demonstration

89

Figure 6-5: Competency-Driven Technological and Non-technological Approaches

Competency-Driven	Technology Techniques	Non-technology Techniques
Assign coach or mentor	• Online mentoring program • Online coaching program	• Phone • Coaching forums (classroom) • Mentoring forums (classroom)
Create a community for mentor and mentee	• E-mails • Chat rooms • Instant messaging	• Study groups
Practice the competency	• Simulation • Discussion forums with report outs to mentor or coach	• Workshops • Personal meetings
Hold discussions	• Discussion forums • Chat rooms with senior leadership • Symposiums	• Workshops • Personal meetings
Resolve uncertainty	• E-mail • Instant messaging	• Personal meetings
Capture learning events	• Knowledge management	• White papers • Lessons-learned documents

The Best Training and Learning Platforms

There is no such thing as a "best" training and learning method, because organizational cultures are not all the same. How does the organization learn? You need to understand this and review the learning model most applicable. After identifying the learning model(s) you will adopt, identify which platforms are best for your training and development strategy. Think about the following:

• *IT structure and support.* Without this, life is hard! Do you have an Internet or intranet capable of supporting the platform?

- *Cost versus benefit.* Can the objectives of the learning event be achieved in a less costly way? Do we have to have classroom delivery to present awareness training? Do we have to use classroom training to introduce concepts, or can a blended approach be used with e-learning and classroom learning? Can we achieve the learning objectives without training, and make it a mentoring role that benefits a manager and an employee?

Use the formula:

$$VALUE = \frac{Benefit}{Cost}$$

- *Time.* How much time are you going to take to deliver the learning? Do the participants have that kind of time available? Most people who attend training hate to be gone from their "normal" routine.

- *Intended audience.* If you have a more seasoned workforce, people are more likely to want to use printed materials versus learn online. Younger workforces tend to enjoy the online learning.

A platform that is effective in one corporation won't necessarily be effective for another. You'll have to work within the confines of the organizational structure and comfort of management. There is always an amount of uncertainty and resistance to change with any organization intervention or change. Be prepared to leverage the corporation's current training, learning, and development strengths, and blend them into your platform strategy.

Platforms and Learning Needs

Once you are familiar with various training and learning platforms, you need to identify your needs, before you determine what platform to use. A needs assessment is a process used to identify and uncover reasons for gaps in performance. Countless managers have come to me saying "I have a training problem." They immediately ask for a training course. That's not the time to build the course—that's the time to ask questions and determine whether or not training is the intervention the client really needs. I'll give you a quick example.

91

A manager notices that a quality-control specialist has not filled in the product shipment log correctly. Of the 40 line items, he has left off several bin numbers and two batch codes. The manager calls the training group together right away and reports that he has a training problem.

This is not a training problem. The employee was able to correctly fill out other line items in the log; this tells me that he has the basic skills, understanding, and ability to fill out the log book correctly. This is really a case where the manager has to do some coaching to find the real problem.

Figure 6-6 is a one-page assessment that you can give to your clients to help you identify learning needs. If clients fill out the one-page assessment, they'll have some sense of ownership in whatever learning intervention they ultimately use. It also helps you weed out situations in which training is not appropriate. The fact that it is a one-page assessment will be attractive to your clients because:

- It is a small investment of time.
- It is easily understood.
- It provides quick insight toward a solution.

Figure 6-6: Client Assessment Form

Self-Assessment

To determine if **training** or other appropriate actions are needed, complete the following form. Place a checkmark in the box for each **_true_** statement.

Subject: _____

1. ☐ This is a new skill for the employee.

2. ☐ The employee is not doing something now that he/she has done successfully in the past.

3. Why do you think training is necessary? *(Check all the items that apply.)*

☐ Taking on new people	☐ Accident records	☐ Customer requirements
☐ New procedures/systems	☐ High turnover of new recruits	☐ Competitors
☐ New standards		☐ Regulations and requirements
☐ New products	☐ Loss of customers	
☐ New customers	☐ Increasing turnover of experienced employees	
☐ New equipment		Other: (please specify)
☐ Substandard evaluations	☐ Standards of work not achieved	
☐ Requests from others	☐ Increase in waste/rejects/errors	_____
☐ Review of training plans (PDP)		_____
☐ Diversification to new markets	☐ Decreases in productivity and output	_____
☐ Succession planning	☐ Employee never performed task	_____
☐ Feedback from other training	☐ New/changes to legislation	_____
☐ Customer complaints		_____

4. ☐ There are already training courses that can satisfy the training need.

5. ☐ There are no training courses currently offered that can satisfy the training need.

Results/Actions	
If you checked . . .	**Do the following . . .**
#1	Go to question #3 and make sure you have circled all the reasons why training is necessary. **NOTE:** Items 1 and 2 cannot both be checked.
#2	You *don't* have a training problem. The employee has been trained. Possibly use a job aid or coaching. **NOTE:** Items 1 and 2 cannot both be checked.
#3	Make sure you have checked all the reasons that apply.
#4	Show people how to get this training. **NOTE:** Items 4 and 5 cannot both be checked.
#5	E-mail, copy, or fax your assessment to the Training Group. Please include your name and phone number. **NOTE:** Items 4 and 5 cannot both be checked.

93

If the one-page client assessment shows that there might be a training deficiency, use Figure 6-7 to begin the process of designing a training intervention. Both forms should be available to corporate university clients.

Figure 6-7: Training Intervention Planner

Training Intervention Planner

Training Topic Information

Training Topic: _____

Analysis

What's happening in the organization that might be a trigger for training needs analysis? Check all that apply.

Systems/Processes and Job Design

☐ New system	☐ New policy/procedure	☐ New process
☐ System upgrade	☐ Policy/procedural change	☐ New product
☐ System reliability	☐ Regulatory requirement	☐ New equipment
☐ Competency changes	☐ Developmental program changes	☐ Skill requirements

Leadership and Management

☐ Taking on new people	☐ Productivity decrease	☐ Increased waste
☐ High turnover	☐ Cost escalations	☐ Customer complaint
☐ Employee performance	☐ Training feedbacks	☐ Poor product quality
☐ New customers	☐ Accident recordables	☐ Downsizing group
☐ High absentee rates	☐ Employee conflicts	☐ Job requirements
☐ Increased downtime	☐ Request from management	
☐ Poor work standards		

Organizational Change

☐ New organizational structure	☐ Climate survey analysis	☐ Six-Sigma project results
	☐ Diversify to new markets	☐ Business model change
☐ Reengineering effort	☐ Workout (Kaizen)	☐ Lean production
☐ Other (please describe)		

_____

_____

Check the appropriate response box for each of the following questions or statements.

What target group would the training be for?	☐ New employees	☐ Existing employees
Is this a new skill for this group?	☐ Yes	☐ No
If this is a new skill, does it require . . .	☐ New procedures?	☐ New knowledge?
Does every member of the target group need training?	☐ Yes	☐ No

(continued)

Figure 6-7: Training Intervention Planner (continued)

If this is not a new skill, what are the members of this target group *not* doing that they should be doing?

_____

_____

_____

_____

If this is not a new skill, what is the current knowledge level in the area to be trained?

_____

_____

_____

If not all members of the target group need the training, who will be participating?

_____

_____

_____

Who is sponsoring the training?

_____

_____

_____

Who are the subject matter experts who can help with course information?

_____

_____

_____

_____

Does the Safety group need to be involved?	☐ Yes	☐ No	
Do you need to coordinate with the Legal department?	☐ Yes	☐ No	

What training tools already exist for members of the target group that might help them?

_____

_____

_____

_____

(continued)

Figure 6-7: Training Intervention Planner *(continued)*

Is there a supporting task analysis document already in existence?   ☐ Yes   ☐ No
(Attach Task Analysis report)

Is training the best solution given the identified triggers?   ☐ Yes   ☐ No
(Explain why or why not)

_____

_____

_____

_____

_____

_____

_____

_____

_____

_____

_____

_____

_____

_____

_____

_____

_____

_____

_____

If training is not the best solution, STOP HERE.

If training is the best approach, check the analysis approach determination you have decided to use. Make sure the correct blended learning approaches are listed in the next section.

☐ Skills-driven approach (identify gaps in knowledge and skills)

☐ Attitude-driven approach (identify process and behavioral issues for situations)

☐ Competency-driven approach (transfer knowledge while observed)

☐ Organizational approach (identify problems of Organizational Development)

(continued)

Figure 6-7: Training Intervention Planner *(continued)*

Planning Section

Fill in the following information for each training objective.

Training Objective	Learning Platform*	Evaluation Criteria	Measurement Effectiveness**	How will it be measured?

97

(continued)

Figure 6-7: Training Intervention Planner *(continued)*

* Check the kinds of learning you intend to use and make sure each is listed in the Learning Platform column.

☐ Video	☐ Classroom instruction	☐ Job aids
☐ CD-ROM (stand-alone)	☐ DVD	☐ E-learning
☐ Webinars	☐ Pre-Work requirement	☐ OJT checklists
☐ Assign mentors	☐ Assign coach	☐ Simulations
☐ Post training assignment	☐ Attend seminar/	☐ Self-study books/
☐ Job shadowing	symposium	materials

**Check every organizational need that has been identified and make sure it is listed in the Measurement Effectiveness column.

☐ Decrease operating costs	☐ Increase in sales
☐ Decrease downtime	☐ Increase in productivity
☐ Decrease in employee turnover	☐ Increase in operating profit
☐ Decrease manual operation or interface	☐ Increase customer base
☐ Decrease waste (lost production)	☐ Increase repeat customers
☐ Decrease customer complaints	☐ Increase cost avoidance
☐ Decrease quality incidents	☐ Increase tool use in projects
☐ Decrease employee injuries	☐ Increase skill set
☐ Decrease cycle time	
☐ Decrease financial spending	
☐ Decrease time to competency	

☐ Others:

_____

_____

Who will develop training tools?   ☐ Internal   ☐ Vendor   ☐ Both

If vendor, list company, contact person, and phone/cell/fax numbers.

_____

_____

_____

_____

_____

_____

_____

(continued)

Figure 6-7: Training Intervention Planner *(concluded)*

Training Rollout

What is the date for the pilot session?

_____

_____

Who will attend this session?

_____

_____

_____

What is the deadline date for finalizing the training materials?

_____

_____

What is the date for training/program implementation?

_____

_____

Describe the rollout plan.

_____

_____

_____

_____

_____

_____

_____

_____

_____

_____

99

Scorecard Measurement

What level of measurement (Kirkpatrick) will be collected in the training scorecard?

☐ Level I
☐ Level II
☐ Level III
☐ Level IV

Chapter 7

Knowledge Management and the University

What is meant by *knowledge management*? Knowledge management refers to the focus of enabling organizations to share the intelligence of their work and related work processes. The ultimate goal of knowledge management is to advance organizational learning by strengthening competencies throughout the organization. The system helps you understand how to locate, share, and use the information effectively. Knowledge yields value when the people know where it is and how they can get it, know that it will help them through proven results, and are committed to keeping it current and useful. The key benefits of knowledge management (KM) are:

· *KM improves staff efficiency.* Support staff for a call center will be able to search the knowledge base for answers, allowing them to reduce the time it takes to answer customer questions. It should also help them work as a more efficient and cohesive team.

· *KM reduces training costs.* KM reduces the training time for new employees, and lowers the costs by utilizing blended learning approaches. The knowledge base provides information instantly for employees who need it.

· *Information can be shared and reused.* KM provides a systematic way for sharing and reusing knowledge. It also allows employees to share knowledge they know personally.

- *KM improves performance consistency.* By standardizing responses to the customer, an organization can streamline its efforts to maximize time, reduce confusion, and build tighter relationships internally and with clients.

Considering the benefits an organization derives from managing its collective knowledge, you would think KM would be welcomed and embraced by leadership and cascaded down throughout the organization. That doesn't always happen, largely due to the inability to standardize KM in the organization. A corporation relies on its technology to standardize KM. In most cases, the technology is so new and robust that it can't be supported throughout the entire organization (except perhaps to some business units, with the right infrastructure). KM is *not* technology, but it can be done by taking the existing technologies, organization, training platforms, OD interventions, policies, and procedures, and placing them into one informal platform to gain a competitive advantage.

How can a corporate university be used to share knowledge? First, you need to assess the current infrastructure and review informal methods of learning possible in that environment. One of the most common informal environments is the e-community, which should be accessed through the university. Message boards, threaded discussions on best practices and how results were obtained, frequently asked questions (FAQs), and other chat environments such as instant messaging are part of an e-community.

Figure 7-1 presents a simple strategy used to create, distribute, and apply knowledge to drive the value of knowledge management throughout the organization.

Figure 7-1: A Basic KM Model

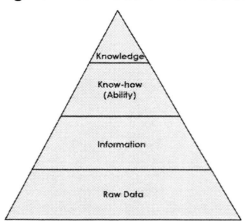

Data Collection

Data is the foundation of organizational knowledge—the observable facts that make up any organizational learning event, formal or informal. The university should house and directly or indirectly support major pieces of data collected. Figure 7-2 presents a few of the more common areas for data collection. Some of these can be launched and collected from the corporate university.

Figure 7-2: Data Collection

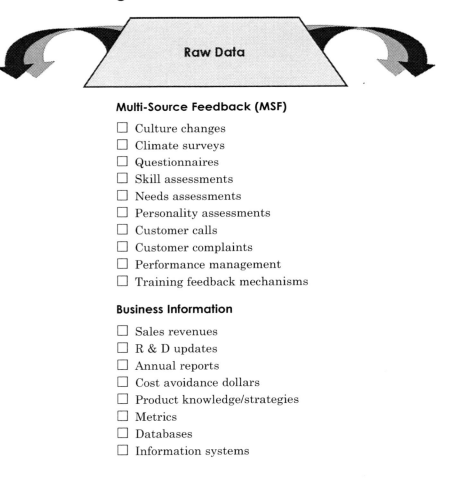

Multi-Source Feedback (MSF)

☐ Culture changes
☐ Climate surveys
☐ Questionnaires
☐ Skill assessments
☐ Needs assessments
☐ Personality assessments
☐ Customer calls
☐ Customer complaints
☐ Performance management
☐ Training feedback mechanisms

Business Information

☐ Sales revenues
☐ R & D updates
☐ Annual reports
☐ Cost avoidance dollars
☐ Product knowledge/strategies
☐ Metrics
☐ Databases
☐ Information systems

Information in this context refers to the data that is taken from sources and put into some meaningful form or usability. In order for any information to take on a meaningful form or be used as a critical success factor, it must align with indicators measured by business units and supported by the university. Figure 7-3 provides examples of information alignment.

Figure 7-3: Meaningful Information

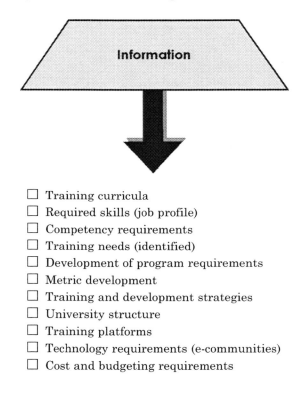

☐ Training curricula
☐ Required skills (job profile)
☐ Competency requirements
☐ Training needs (identified)
☐ Development of program requirements
☐ Metric development
☐ Training and development strategies
☐ University structure
☐ Training platforms
☐ Technology requirements (e-communities)
☐ Cost and budgeting requirements

Know-how refers to the application of information and data from various sources and continuous experiences to achieve competencies (i.e., what it looks like when a competency is being consistently utilized to its fullest potential). Figure 7-4 provides examples of know-how.

Figure 7-4: Know-How and Knowledge

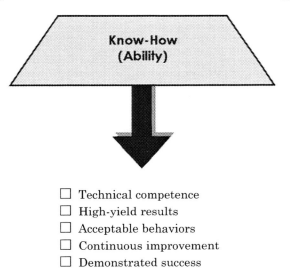

☐ Technical competence
☐ High-yield results
☐ Acceptable behaviors
☐ Continuous improvement
☐ Demonstrated success

105

Knowledge is gained when information is combined with know-how and aligned with competencies, key objectives, and goals of the corporation.

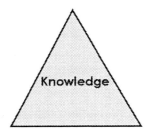

Chapter 8

Aligning Training and Development

Chapter 7 explained what knowledge management is and described the role it plays in the university. How we align that knowledge into the university and provide training and development opportunities is the focus of this chapter. Competencies, criteria, and desired behaviors have to be aligned to bridge gaps. The university cannot effectively reach its goals without a people-development model, however. (Remember, the university exists to support the growth and development of all people.) It will allow you to effectively identify the behaviors and competencies the organization needs if it is to remain competitive far into the future. Figure 8-1 illustrates how a basic people-development model works.

Figure 8-1: A Basic People-Development Model

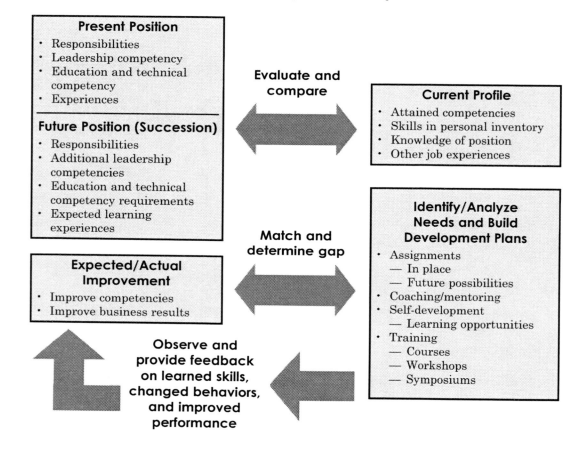

In the following managerial and non-managerial examples, we've already identified competencies related to the job description, criteria, and sample behaviors. Now we need to identify supporting training modules and development opportunities. The managerial skill tables have been divided into three groups. An example of the Managerial and Supervisory skill table is also provided here.

- Competencies (Managerial and Supervisory)
- Administrative
- Product

Managerial and Supervisory Competencies: Skill Table			
Competency	**Sample Behaviors**	**Bridging the Gap**	
		Available Training Courses in University	**Sample Development Opportunities**
Manage Work Processes	• Demonstrates high degree of adaptability and works effectively through difficult and ambiguous situations • Applies strong personal learning skills across multiple situations • Demonstrates good first impression, commands respect, and has confidence • Offers prompt action in accomplishing objectives; takes action beyond what's required • Assumes responsibility and accountability for objectives	• Decision-making Fundamentals • Problem-solving Fundamentals • Interpersonal Effectiveness • Root Cause Analysis • Conducting/Holding Meetings • Technical Training Courses • Facilitating Change • Taking Initiative • Project Management • Six-Sigma Courses	• Play key role in emergency production, financial, or distribution situations • Facilitate meetings • Lead Six-Sigma projects • Develop or implement plans to control or decrease operating costs • Set up and lead a team • Complete a project with tight time constraints • Determine root causes of problems and execute action plans
Inspiring Others to Perform and Getting Work Done through Others	• Successfully assists teams and others by using formal and informal skills • Focuses and guides others in accomplishing work objectives • Ensures sufficient follow-up of delegated work and utilizes the skills of others • Uses appropriate interpersonal skills to reach goals and address needs and potential of others • Makes sure that flow of information is accurate and timely • Contributes to team as an active member; uses skills to develop the team	• Coaching • Teamwork Fundamentals • Virtual Teams • Coaching Basics • Delegation • Interpersonal Effectiveness • Leadership Fundamentals • Developing High Performance Teams • Effective Communication Mentoring • Team Performance Planning	• Set up and lead a new team • Share ownership in problem-solving projects • Be a mentor • Face a situation outside the technical expertise and rely on leadership skills to solve • Participate in a Six-Sigma project led by someone else • Sponsor a Six-Sigma project as a stakeholder

109

(continued)

Managerial and Supervisory Competencies: Skill Table *(concluded)*			
		Bridging the Gap	
Competency	**Sample Behaviors**	**Available Training Courses in University**	**Sample Development Opportunities**
Managing Diverse People and Dealing with Conflict	• Understands how to develop and maintain productive relationships • Demonstrates effective skills in building and maintaining "customer" relationships • Interacts in a way that others in conflict have confidence in their intentions and builds support toward goals • Uses communication skills (verbal and written) to seek understanding, gain agreement, and develop a positive work environment • Negotiates by exploring alternatives and other positions to reach outcomes and wins support of all parties • Manages conflict to reduce tension; resolves conflict; creates and maintains a positive environment	• Building Trust • Communicating with Others • Guiding Conflict Resolution • Influencing Others • Resolving Team Conflict • Valuing Differences • Communicating and Listening	• Interact with external customers on a Voice of the Customer Project • Help with employee or customer problems; hear people out and capture views • Follow up with a customer regarding service, and help them address/solve problems • Lead a cross-functional Six-Sigma project • Participate in interviewing and hiring
Becoming Organization Savvy and Managing Work Processes	• Achieves business results by effectively structuring and carrying out work • Identifies opportunities and takes action to build relationships among self, team, and other functions • Originates action plans to improve existing conditions and processes • Identifies opportunity areas, implements solutions, and measures impact • Identifies/understands problems and can generate sufficient data from multiple sources • Accomplishes tasks by considering all involved; understands implications of work on others' work	• Making Decisions • Planning and Organizing • Problem-Solving Fundamentals • Time Management • Business Finance: Time Value of Money • Financials for Non-Financial Professionals • Succeeding as a New Manager	• Develop and write a Business Case • Lead a cross-functional Six-Sigma project • Develop or implement plans to control or decrease operating costs • Play a role in the cross-functional business initiative • Take part in the negotiation and administration of union contracts and/or hear union grievances

Employee Skills Inventory

We provided a basic skills table for managerial and supervisory skills, but what about non-management employees? Basically, it's the same model. However, the skill requirements will contain more depth than breadth.

Human Interaction: Skill Table			
Competency	Sample Behaviors	Bridging the Gap	
		Available Training Courses in University	Sample Development Opportunities
Demonstrate Flexibility	• Expresses self and demonstrates values • Demonstrates a degree of adaptability and works effectively with others • Takes action in accomplishing objectives • Demonstrates high work standards	• Interpersonal Effectiveness	• Take a team role in a Six-Sigma project • Take part in a project with time constraints
Communicate	• Capable of and uses some informal leadership skills • Uses relationships to accomplish goals • Uses communication skills (verbal and written) to seek understanding and accomplish tasks • Demonstrates ability to successfully interact with others	• Communicating with Others • Valuing Differences • Communicating and Listening • Teamwork Fundamentals • Interpersonal Effectiveness • Effective Communication • Listening Skills	• Interact with external customers on a team • Coordinate with a sales representative in response to customer needs/wants/desires
Results	• Identifies opportunities to build team relationships to help achieve goals • Uses contacts and knowledge to meet local or plant-level needs	• Partnerships: Creating Synergy • Problem-Solving Fundamentals • Teamwork Fundamentals	• Co-develop or co-implement plans to control or decrease operating costs

111

Technical Skills: Table				
Competency	Criteria	Sample Behaviors	**Bridging the Gap**	
			Available Training Courses in University	Sample Development Opportunities
Making Decisions	Operations Skills	• Assesses daily operations and operational requirements • Demonstrates knowledge about operation at all levels • Assesses the operation of all equipment • Takes appropriate actions to optimize equipment • Demonstrates knowledge about equipment • Effectively communicates to higher echelons regarding operational requirements • Demonstrates knowledge in business decision making associated with daily operations • Can explain the operation process step by step	Operations 101	• Participate in the startup and shutdown of equipment • Go on deliveries with a driver • Participate in an internal quality audit

Product Skills: Table				
Competency	Criteria	Sample Behaviors	**Bridging the Gap**	
			Available Training Courses in University	Sample Development Opportunities
Understand the Business	Product Knowledge	• Understands and explains facts about on-site product(s) • Can explain the properties associated with the product(s) • Understands and explains customer uses of the product(s) • Understands all potential safety concerns associated with the product(s)	• Product Handling training modules • Product Information sheets • Home page product information • List of customers that use specific products and how they use them	• Explain product properties and uses • Take part in a current product being used for or in a new application

Chapter 9

Staffing the Corporate University

We've talked about why and how to create a corporate university and explored various function and support considerations. Now we get to the costs related to staffing. In my benchmarking and comparison studies, I've come across all the extremes. The university requires a balanced staff of qualified people, as well as strategy. Before you can determine what level of staffing you'll need, let's look at three options:

- A "controlled" university
- A "partnered" university
- An outsourced university

The Controlled University

A controlled university is one that is fully supported by internal staff: instructors, complete IT support, instructional designers, materials design, shipping, printing, administration, OD, Webmasters, subject matter experts (SMEs), and internally developed and designed LMS/LCMS. Several corporate universities are set up this way.

The best way to staff the university is to determine how it fits into the overall corporation's strategy and identify which programs and functions will need the most attention. Some of the corporate universities I've researched have as many as 60 staff members, while others have as few as eight.

Figure 9-1 illustrates a typical structure for a "controlled" university. I'm not recommending this organizational layout; I'm merely presenting information collected over the years. Figure 9-2 presents the pros and cons of this strategy. If you are aware of the downside, you can take steps to avoid the traps.

Figure 9-1: Organizational Structure for a Controlled University (example)

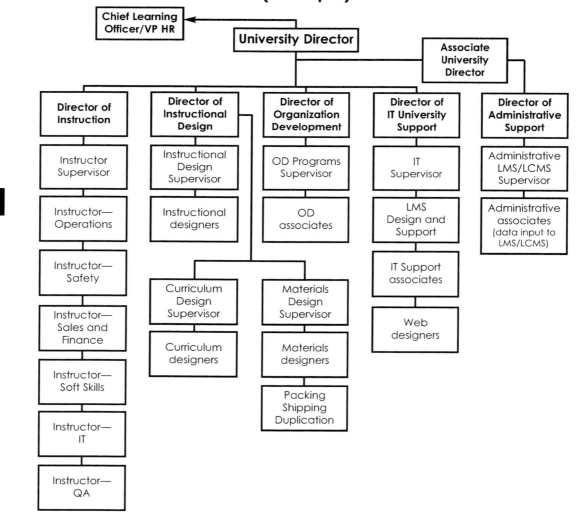

Figure 9-2: Pros and Cons of a Controlled University

The Controlled University	
Pro	**Con**
Tighter controls/processes within the university	• Tighter controls and processes will eventually lead to negligible idea growth for the university. • Tighter controls can lead to creation of silos in the university (e.g., instructors don't teach the course the way it was designed). • Changes may be difficult to "sell" to the internal university team and thus less likely to be implemented—leads to a possible loss of competitive advantage.
Internal products specifically designed for organization	• Using internal products will most likely cost more time and dollars to implement versus using off-the-shelf products with minor tweaking or using them as is.
Ability to cross-utilize resources with input to project priorities	• High salary requirements • High employee count associated to a function that normally doesn't create income
Most problems are within the control of the university	• Employee skills become too specialized and not diversified for continued employee growth and development
Roadblocks to problems can be overcome quickly	• Possibility of the "blame game" comes to the forefront if groups become siloed within the university

115

The Partnered University

The partnered university is supported by internal employees. However, there are a few key external partners that provide one or more of the following: instructional design, administration, Web design and development and Web support, subject matter experts (SME), LMS/LCMS companies, material design, instructors, shipping, and so on. The specific design of the partnered university depends on cost, internal skills, current system applications, and, of course, the budget.

The most effective way to begin staffing the partnered university is to first determine how it fits into the overall corporate strategy and identify which programs and functions need to be continually developed and retained in-house. This is the most common set-up, as most partners are reputable LMS providers.

Figure 9-3 presents an example of an organizational approach associated with this strategy. Your organizational chart might be completely different, depending on the factors identified in the previous paragraph.

Figure 9-4 presents several pros and cons of this partnered approach. It doesn't mean they will happen if the foresight and awareness are present.

Figure 9-3: Organizational Structure for a Partnered University (example)

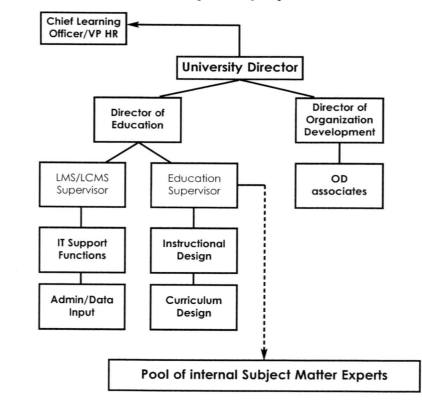

Figure 9-4: Pros and Cons of a Partnered University

The Partnered University	
Pro	**Con**
• Using a few key strategic partners allows flexibility to utilize a smaller number of skilled employees • Dollar savings using partners (versus full staffing)	• Software changes and upgrades are based on major industry trends that may not align with corporate strategies • Software incompatibility and problems are not within the total control of the university, and take time and money to correct if the maintenance contract isn't procured
• Wide range of products and solutions available	• Reliance on off-the-shelf products to meet specific requirements . • External products not designed for a specific organizational need without incurring additional costs
• Ability to benchmark and compare latest trends and industry practices without additional investment	• Limited to the strategic partners' current client lists
• Fewer instructors need to be associated with the university	• Heavy reliance on subject matter experts increases time to push out product • Most SMEs are not qualified instructors

117

The Outsourced University

The outsourced university is supported by a handful of internal employees. Key external partners provide the LMS/LCMS product, instructional design, administration, Web development and support, material design, instructors, shipping, and even SMEs. Corporations of every size use this totally outsourced set-up. It's assumed that the corporate strategy and functions are not retained in-house.

This is normally the least costly approach, but it should only be considered if the corporation has very few product lines and/or services. The more product lines and services a corporation has, the greater specialization that will be required. When business units within the corporation perceive that their needs are not being met, they are highly likely to develop and staff their own in-house training unit, which will increase internal costs.

You might have a strong relationship with your outsourced university partners, but be aware that changes and tweaks to training and development programs will come with a high price tag. This is because they offer basic or even static display programs; it's simply cheaper to provide a generic training or development program.

Figure 9-5 presents an example of an organizational approach associated with this strategy.

Figure 9-6 presents several pros and cons of using this strategy. Don't let the list of cons discourage you from using this approach; just take preventative measures when you do your planning.

Figure 9-5: Organizational Structure for an Outsourced University (example)

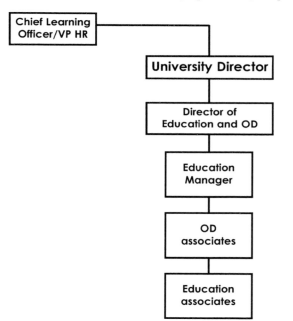

Figure 9-6: Pros and Cons of an Outsourced University

The Outsourced University	
Pro	**Con**
• Having key strategic partners provides flexibility to use a smaller number of skilled employees • Dollar savings using partners (versus full staffing)	• Software changes and upgrades are based on major industry trends that might not align with corporate strategies • Software incompatibility and problems are not within the total control of the university and will take time and money to correct if the maintenance contract isn't procured • Many companies offering outsourcing functions are being purchased by other companies; skills and services can be there one day and gone the next
• Wide range of products and solutions available	• Reliance on off-the-shelf products to meet specific requirements • External products not designed for a specific organizational need without incurring additional costs
• Ability to benchmark and compare latest trends and industry practices, without additional investment	• Limited to the strategic partners' current client lists

Chapter 10

The Small Business University

A small business interested in creating a corporate university must consider several factors that are not applicable to a large company's efforts to do the same thing. Before we get into the various pros and cons, let's define a small business. For our purposes, we'll say it's an organization that has between 50 and 300 employees. Figure 10-1 illustrates pros and cons of a small business establishing its own corporate university.

Figure 10-1: Pros and Cons of Small Business University

Small Business		Large Business	
Pro	Con	Pro	Con
Easier to get information cascaded out to the people			Some complexity in getting information cascaded out to the people
	Only a small number of people are involved (having depth of experiences versus breadth)	Greater number of people to obtain inputs on background information and other ideas. Staff has greater breadth of experiences	

(continued)

Figure 10-1: Pros and Cons of Small Business University *(concluded)*

Small Business		Large Business	
Pro	Con	Pro	Con
	Costs for the university are incurred by a very few or even a single department	Costs for the university can be shared among various business units, so it's less of a "hit" on the budget numbers	
	Less likely to get quantity order discounts	Can take advantage of quantity orders from vendors to get discounts	
Easier to get agreement on what to include in a university, since there is less possibility of silos and political landmines			Harder to get agreement of what should be in a university; you will have to overcome silos and political landmines
Decreased amount of time to get approval because there are fewer numbers of stakeholders			A great deal of time and effort spent getting approval through the high number of stakeholders
Easier to get government funding through grants for training and education if operating in one state			Normally difficult to get government funding through grants, because of the number of locations in different states/countries
Easier to "sell" the university approach			Tougher to sell the approach
Managers and senior leadership will be involved			Normally this is delegated to others in the organization
		Likely to produce revenue from design, development, and sales of training products	

If you are part of a small business, the approach outlined in the previous chapters of this book will work just as well for you as it does for larger organizations. Just pay attention to alignment. In some respects, a small business enjoys certain advantages when establishing a corporate university in all areas except cost. This is where creativity and innovation are particularly important.

Education Grants

State education grants generally provide funding for corporate universities and can help with the training and development that small businesses need. That said, grants take a great deal of time and patience to apply for. There is a lot of paperwork that must go through channels. I highly recommend finding a grantwriter to do this work for you. Grantwriters are aware of what can and cannot be submitted and already have most forms, know the submission channels better than you (as well as the landmines), and are not relatively expensive. Professional grantwriters also know the rules and regulations associated with the grant, and can give you better insight into what information to collect.

If you are considering applying for a state training grant, keep in mind the fact that state grants are for state residents. The grantwriter's costs are normally a very low percentage of the total value of the grant (somewhere between 5 and 10 percent). If you choose not to use a grantwriter, go to your state's government Web site for information regarding training grants for small businesses.

Consortia

If financing is necessary, consider entering into a partnership with an academic institution. Many universities reach out to small businesses in the community. Another way to fund your project is to form a consortium of small businesses. If the corporations and businesses are in the same industry, the consortium can be focused on industry-specific issues.[6]

Learning Model

Small businesses normally follow the skill-driven approach to learning; the majority of learning is done on-the-job. This requires very detailed OJT checklists and the effective use of coaching tools. Unfortunately, many small businesses don't understand this approach and consequently experience higher than normal turnover.

I was once involved in developing a management education program for a service business. Many of the first-line managers' skills needed refinement (and in some cases, introduction). Coaching was one of the program's areas of concentration, and I was amazed to learn that none of the managers had ever heard of OJT checklists and were not familiar with the situational approach to management.

I asked them how they trained new people and what skills they needed to bring to the table. "Everything is done on-the-job, and we really don't expect them to have any skills because the jobs are cleaning, sweeping, landscaping, and janitorial. Most anybody can do that."

"Then what do you expect from the people?" I asked them.
"To show up and do the job."
"To what level?" I asked.
"To our expectation."
"Have you explained what your expectations are?" I asked.

It was as if a light bulb had just switched on. There was a sense of excitement—a sense of *Wow!* and *I get it!* I had each manager create a detailed OJT checklist that employees would be able to follow. I then had the managers review each other's checklists to see if they could do the job if left to themselves. The managers found out one thing very quickly: creating these checklists wasn't as easy as they thought. There had to be some detail about the expectations of the manager and an understanding of the requirements. A sense of pride when the work was completed was also important because the managers were right: There was no guesswork.

One of the other areas of concern this exercise helped alleviate was the amount of time spent on processes that their teams were responsible for. Several of the people performed the jobs differently, which led to a high degree of variation. This variation had to be decreased in order for this company to increase business without adding employees.

I'm not saying the OJT checklists do all of this, but in this case, they provided a starting point, which allowed these managers to begin thinking and acting like managers, rather than workers. They were now free to begin building customer alliances, talking with customers, getting and winning new business. Today, the company is thriving, has received many community awards, and is one of Western New York's top small businesses. That wasn't my doing—it was theirs!

One common mistake many small businesses make regarding corporate universities is that they feel they have to offer everything. They don't. Pick and choose what you need. Determine what makes sense for the business, its culture, and its desire to win.

Chapter 11

Conclusion

It is vital that the corporate university help the corporation execute its short-term and long-term strategies. For a corporate university to be successful, it must fit and be accepted into the organizational culture, directly affect bottom-line results for senior leaders and managers of business units, provide the how-to for the workers, and be easy to use. We've shown you how to align the university with the various needs of the organization, and we've discussed the required partnerships with Human Resources, organizational development, and business unit leaders. Collaboration between these departments is vital to its success: without it, you become mired in mud and it will be next-to-impossible to sell the concept.

The organization has to have a collective thirst for learning. Effectively done, learning will yield innovation, transformation, and competitive strengths for years to come. I expect corporate universities to play a significant role in organizations for the next 20 years; our workforces, as well as our customers, suppliers, and partners, must be connected to knowledge-sharing networks if we want to succeed. Workplace Learning and Performance professionals must continue to expand the speed, flexibility, and rapid execution of learning assets through Learning Management Systems, business tools, search engines, and technologies so that corporate universities can be more connected to the corporate and business unit workforces they serve.

The chapters are designed to sequentially detail how a corporate university can work in your corporate culture. As with any program initiative, the university will only be as strong as the people who use it, but they must in turn provide input to make it more effective, and keep it updated. You'll find that this will not be done overnight; it's going to take time. You'll have to form collaborative relationships and show what the university can deliver to the stakeholders.

You'll probably find yourself having to lead from the middle of the organization. Leading from the middle builds character, knowledge, and relationships, which are all necessary to execute the required success factors. Leading from the middle will turn you into a true leader—one with vision, courage, and commitment.

You may wonder whether or not all of the blood, sweat, and tears put into creating and developing the corporate university will be worth it. Will it really help the business become a learning organization? Will it add value to the business? Will the senior leadership see, understand, and grasp the opportunity? In a word, *yes!*

Part I: Readiness Self-Assessment

Is your organization ready to establish a corporate university? This self-assessment will help you determine that.

Rate each of the following statements with a 1, 2, 3, or 4. When completed with the assessment, add up the letter ratings.

1	2	3	4
Not a true statement	Seldom true	Mostly true	Always true

_____ The HR, OD, and Training departments have a positive working relationship.

_____ The CEO and staff openly support and encourage training and development.

_____ Senior managers are able to distinguish between HR, OD, and Training responsibilities and explain how they are carried out.

_____ Employees are able to distinguish between HR, OD, and Training responsibilities and explain how they are carried out.

_____ There is a single point of contact for business units to get information on training/development.

_____ There are clear internal processes in place for training and development.

_____ The organization has a solid information technology or information systems department to support training/development initiatives.

_____ The organization partners with or uses only a few third-party suppliers for training/development.

_____ The need for a corporate university has been documented (i.e., assessments).

_____ The organization has an intranet/Internet site available for employees.

_____ A training function is not embedded in the hierarchy of separate business units.

_____ Training and development initiatives are linked to key performance indicators (metrics).

_____ The organization uses a documented feedback process to obtain information from employees.

_____ The organization uses or has developed a learning management system.

_____ The corporation runs or sponsors mandatory job-related training courses.

Part I. Rate each of the following statements with a 1, 2, 3, or 4.

1	2	3	4
Not a true statement	Seldom true	Mostly true	Always true

_____ We have a positive working relationship with the organization's Training, OD, and HR departments.

_____ Our senior managers can explain importance of the Training department.

_____ We use the Training functional group/department as single point of contact to obtain information on training and development.

_____ There are clear processes and products in place that show clients obtain training and development.

_____ There is a single place to go to obtain information about training and development opportunities.

_____ We currently use third-party suppliers for training and development.

_____ We use intranet/Internet sites for internal employee training and development.

_____ We have a separate functional group for training embedded in our organization.

_____ We use training and development initiatives/programs and link them to key performance indicators.

_____ We use a documented feedback process to obtain information from employees about training and development opportunities.

_____ We use a learning management system (purchased or internally developed) to track and provide training/development opportunities.

28

(Part II and Part III are on next page.)

Part II. Place a ✔ next to each item you would like to see included in a corporate university. Use the additional space at the bottom of the form for your own suggestions.

☐ Access to online training modules (e-Learning)

☐ Information about instructor-led courses

☐ Information about performance management programs

☐ Information about HR programs (diversity and harassment)

☐ Access first-line supervisory training modules

☐ Information about career ladders

☐ Competency information

☐ Training curriculums

☐ Six-Sigma and workout programs

☐ Coaching tools

☐ Financial training modules

☐ Corporate metrics

☐ Newsletters

☐ Best Practices information

☐ Skill assessments

☐ Articles about leadership and development

☐ Technical training modules and assessments

☐ 360°-feedback programs

☐ Problem solvers (names and numbers)

Suggestions: _____

_____

Part III. Rate each of the following statements with a 1, 2, 3, or 4.

1	2	3 .	4
Not a true statement	Seldom true	Mostly true	Always true

_____ I would use a corporate university if the items I selected in Part II were included in it.

_____ I would use a corporate university if it is user friendly and easy to get to.

_____ I would make time to use a corporate university if the items I selected in Part II were included in it.

_____ I would use the training and development opportunities provided by a corporate university for development planning if the items I selected in Part II were included in it.

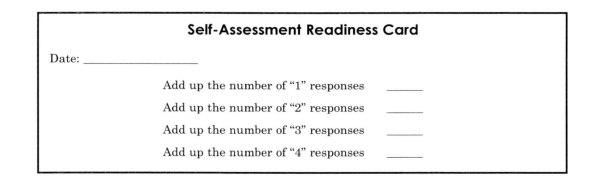

Interview Guide

Name of individual being interviewed: _____ Date: _____

Questions	Prompts and Probes for Questions

Project Roles and Responsibilities			
Project Function	Answerable to	Responsible to	Collaborate with

Project Plan Outline				
Item #	Activity	Deliverable	Responsibility	Milestone

Customer Support Requirements				
Customer Code	Product or Service	Customer Support Requirement	Quality Indicator (to include metrics)	Expected Performance Level

KPI Alignment			
KPI	Key Process	Critical Success Factor (CSF)	Current Capability

135

SWOT Analysis				
Key Processes	Strengths	Weaknesses	Opportunities	Threats

References

1. Kirkpatrick, D. (1998). *Evaluating training programs* (2nd Ed.). San Francisco, CA: Berrett-Kohler Publishers.

2. Waclawski, J., & Church, A. (2002). *Organization development: A data-driven approach to organizational change.* San Francisco, CA: Jossey-Bass Publishers.

3. Martin, P., & Tate, K. (1997). *Project management memory jogger.* Salem, NH: Goal/QPC.

4. Hiam, A. (2003). *Strategic leadership type indicator.* Amherst, MA: HRD Press, Inc.

5. Welch, J. (2005). *Winning.* New York: HarperCollins Publishers.

6. Allen, M. (2002). *The corporate university handbook.* American Management Association: AMACOM.

About the Author

Jeff Grenzer currently designs, develops, and executes intervention strategies and organizational development programs for organizations that want to align short-term execution and long-term growth corporate strategies.

He is a frequent speaker and writer on performance improvement and technology, and has taught graduate, undergraduate, and teacher-training courses in leadership development, strategic planning and execution, learning productivity, educational development, and supervisory skills. Listed in the 2004–2005 United Who's Who Registry of Executives and Professionals, Jeff has written articles for the International Society of Performance Improvement online magazine *Performance Express* and developed training and developmental programs for several Fortune 300 companies, The University of New York—Buffalo, and several small businesses. He has taught rapid deployment logistics systems and weapon system capabilities for international personnel and commissioned and conducted competitive sourcing and privatization studies for the United States Air Force.

Jeff has an MBA in Business and an OD Certification from the University of New York—Buffalo, a master's degree in Human Resources Management, a teaching certification from the Southern Association of Colleges, and a bachelor's degree in marketing and management from Western Illinois University. He is also a Certified Performance Technologist with the International Society for Performance Improvement.